The Unique Cut Diamond

CHRISTINE ROACHE-HAGLEY

The Unique Cut Diamond

Copyright © 2021 **Christine Roache-Hagley**

All rights reserved. Printed in the United States of America

No part of this book may be used or reproduced in any manner whatsoever without written permission except in the case of brief quotations embodied in critical articles or reviews.

ISBN: 9798752516504

Published by: Daughter of the King Publishing

Christine Roache-Hagley

The author was born in the Rexdale neighbourhood of Toronto, but later moved to Malton where she spent most of her childhood years. She is the eldest of four children on her mother's side, and is child number nine for her father. Diagnosed with a learning disability at a tender age, she struggled to stay afloat in the traditional school system and attended a Blended Approach School in her late teen years where she successfully graduated. Christine is now a Community-Based Counsellor working with At-Risk Youth, in the Customer Service Sector. She is a proud mother of a beautiful four year old daughter.

"I listen to understand; I know how to decipher people's emotions."

"There is an advantage in anything you do."

"Even though I was faced with all these obstacles and challenges in my life, I never gave up because I always see the light in every

situation; whether I was angry or sad, I always knew there was more to me than the situation I was in at the time."

theuniquecutdiamond@gmail.com

Introduction

I wrote this book because I felt I needed to share my story with the world because it is truly unique. It took me a while to write this book because of the trials in my life that I went through and because of my anger. I struggled with the decision and even burned all of my jottings, but I never gave up, and now I want my story to be told more than ever before-raw, unfiltered, withholding nothing, just me. In order for me to truly live my best life, I had to write this book. It was imperative for me to get this weight off my shoulders.

I never saw much of a highlight in my life. People always encouraged me to write a book. I looked at them and thought, "they are joking." I thought all the abuse, trauma and pain I had to go through was something many other people were going through. It never quite occurred to me that there was anything spectacular about my life that would make the pages of a real book, but I am now looking at things differently. Childhood is supposed to be a happy time; when you want to be around people and when you're supposed to feel loved. It is one of the best times in a person's life. For me it was more misery than childhood.

If there is one thing I've known about myself since childhood, it is that my love never changed regardless of what I went through or what I endured. I always had love for people. I wrote this book because I felt I needed to share my story with the world because unlike every other, this story is unique. This is my truth.

Dedication

I would like to dedicate this book to my Grandmother, my Daughter and my future children.

To my grandmother: Thank you for everything that you've done for me. Without you, I would never be the woman that I am today. I would have never overcome all of life's obstacles had it not been for your faith in me, and your constant encouragement and love.

Table of Contents

Chapter 1 – Who am I?   1

Chapter 2 – Ice bath   13

Chapter 3 – Elements of me   28

Chapter 4 – Torture   38

Chapter 5 – Stolen identity   54

Chapter 6 - My mother's curse   70

Chapter 7 – Length of attention   81

Chapter 8 – Men before your children   90

Chapter 9 – Where it all began   103

Chapter 10 – Guardian angel   109

Chapter 11 – Super hero   119

Chapter 12 - Pride strength & love   124

CHAPTER 1

WHO AM I?

I was born and raised in Toronto- the Rexdale neighbourhood to be specific- was where I spent my early years before moving to Malton. Malton is where my childhood really unfolded. I am of mixed heritage. My mother is from Jamaica and my father is Grenadian. My paternal grandparents are from Scotland which gives me Caribbean and European blood. On my mom's side there are four of us and I am the eldest. Being the eldest of four was rough growing up. I lived with my mom and step dad (which is my brother's father). I had a father but he didn't really play a part in my life until I was sixteen years old. So I was raised by my sister's dad who I refer to as my father. On my biological dad's side there are ten of us and I am the second youngest. I have a younger sister who was born after me. We grew up in many different areas and I bounced around from place to place. It was difficult for me to really stay put because we were always moving. It was either changing schools or neighbourhoods.

My mom and dad are practically the same people. They showed their love in their own way and it wasn't really through me, it was through each other. I don't mean being together; it was just their individual personalities. If I needed something she would call him and he was somewhat there, but it was not like your typical co-parenting scheme. I met my Dad at sixteen so I was already grown. I really did not need anything most of the time, except when there was a school trip or I wanted clothes or a pair of shoes. Generally, there was not much of a demand for him on a regular basis. I thought he was supposed to be there for back-up and support. Whatever role my mom didn't fulfil, my Grandmother or my Aunt would take on in her place. My Mom and my Dad's relationship was very toxic. From what I heard growing up, my Dad was very controlling and manipulative. My Mom wanted her own way and my Dad was abusive. Wasn't really much of a relationship. Then they had me.

The neighbourhood I grew up in was deemed At-Risk because of the pervasive gun violence. I do not remember much except for the fact that we lived in a house and we moved into the basement. I used to play with the landlord's kids and grandkids. So I had friends to play with. It was just me and my mom, and I was the new kid on the block. It was my sister's dad who helped raise me. With him, there was more of a schedule. I had: nannies, certain programs I would participate in, a lot of clothes and every toy in the world. Because of my sister's dad, I had an extended family who embraced me from the time I was two months old. My dad took off after I was born.

On my mom's side there are four of us and I am the eldest. On my dad's side there are ten of us and I am the second youngest. Then there is my younger sister who was born after me. I don't have much of a relationship with my brothers; it is more like I am there, you are there. However, I have a great relationship with my sister on my dad's side. We are very close. We are a year apart so there is commonality in terms of age and shared interests. We met when I was thirteen. I grew up not knowing who my father was, so that relationship was strange to me- but the more I got to know her, the more I got to see that we are not that different from each other.

She has been through the whole dirt with me and my mom. She knows everything about my Mom because she was there. Also, she knows a lot about our Dad because we had similar stories. One particular thing that stands out to me is that when we first met I was just amazed. I did not know much about my Dad's background- so when I found out that I had an older sister, someone that I could look up to, it was a phenomenon. As a child having an older sister made me ecstatic. I had an older sibling who could put me in check and watch out for me. Finally there was someone I could talk to. I did not have that as a child growing up. I felt alone, but when I found her I stopped feeling like that. I knew I had a whole other human being- somebody that I could share a bond with and someone with whom I could share my whole life story. She had the opportunity to get to know the real me, the loving, caring person that I am.

Later when I met my dad's kids we would do sleepovers, go out to lunch and talk on the phone. There were times when we shared different books, ideas and a host of other cool stuff with each other. Because of my sister, I got to experience a whole other lifestyle and family. We went to the movies, the beach, and much more. We did so much together as sister, and I had a life I never had with my siblings on my Mom's side.

When it comes to describing the relationship I have with my mom's kids, I would say my sister and I are somewhat close. The relationship with my brothers is more so based on what I can do for them. It isn't really a relationship. They know they have a sister, and if they need something, they ask. Otherwise they don't speak to me for weeks or sometimes for months. My siblings are brainwashed and emotionally controlled by my mom, so the way they act doesn't surprise me. Yeah. I don't blame them much because of our warped upbringing.

At a young age I was tasked with: cooking, cleaning and taking care of my younger sister and brothers. Come to think of it, I was more of the nanny and housekeeper and less of a child in my home. It is painful not being able to just be a child. I was always being told to do this or do that. "Do this for your brother" or "Do this for me", so I didn't have a childhood. The memories of what I endured are equally painful. There was barely any time for me to go outside and play, or to run around like normal kids because I was always taking care of my brothers and sister.

I don't have the best relationship with my mother. She is totally responsible for a lot of things that have happened in my life. My brothers and my sister were young so they didn't know and understand what was happening. They just knew that I was the one taking care of them. At the age of nine, I was already washing, cleaning and watching my siblings. I was often left home alone at a very young age. I've watched my mom go through abusive relationships while the police came in and out of our lives. It keeps coming back to me how many times I was cheated out of just being a child. It was because I had to do whatever everyone wanted me to do. That included: preparing a meal, cleaning and the ever risky task of taking on the adventures of my brothers and sister. In a nutshell, I was to be their caregiver.

My whole youthful life I was a caregiver, so I see myself as a superhero. Whatever anybody asked me to do, as long as I understood the task and what it entailed, I would get it done.

My mom was always comparing me to my siblings. She would say, "If you can't figure it out yourself, then let your brothers and sister help you." That made me feel some type of way because I'm the oldest, and there were certain things I should've known that I didn't. It wasn't my fault. As a result, I had to lean on my younger siblings for help with a lot of things. This was emotionally scarring for me and I spent many nights crying. When I explained things that I couldn't do, for instance, when I struggled in school, she would automatically assume that I didn't want to do the work and that I was lazy. I just didn't know how to and I didn't know why. I was a child, not a Child Psychologist.

It was my grandmother and my teachers-many of the African-Canadian Educators who understood that it wasn't my lack of effort. They tried to help as best as they could. However, my grandmother was the one who noticed I was struggling and took me to a therapist. She was the one who made them assess me. While I was there, I did an exam and she paid from her pocket. She made sure that I got the help that I needed. After I was diagnosed with a learning disability, she got me into a special school which operated programs related to my development. My mother didn't concern herself with my disability, so my grandmother would always call and try to advise her about the right actions to take to assist me. She was just obstinate and uncaring. All my mother kept saying was that I should learn to do things by myself. Basically, as long as I was in her household, I was on my own.

Because of my learning disability, life was very challenging. It could be the reason that I am slower at learning certain things. It would take repetition and a method of constructivism for me to grasp particular activities. For this reason, visual demonstrations would have greatly assisted my growth. Yet, my mom allowed her lack of knowledge about my learning disability to create a continuous source of discontent and disconnect between us. She looked at me as if I was retarded or stupid. All I required from my mother was patience and a dedication to helping me to comprehend what she tried to communicate to me. She did a poor job and that only made matters worse. I didn't know why I couldn't follow her instructions a lot of the time, and neither did she. Eventually I grew to understand my situation but she didn't even try. My mother had absolutely no patience. It was either you got it or you didn't, and she didn't really care to sit and try with me.

My mother always gave me tasks to accomplish with no instructions. Being a mother now, I think back to the little things that I thought a mother should do- things she clearly missed. There was no nurture or care to support me with strategies to help me learn, grow and function. As soon as she found out that I had a learning disability she wrote me off as stupid. She didn't see the value in me or the purpose of my existence.

I got beat for things that I didn't understand. Things like: multiplication, addition, subtraction and even spelling were reasons I was hit. On Fridays I would get multiplication charts with tables from one to ten that I had to study. Then, I would have to recite them to her by the next Friday, and if I didn't know something, I would get hit with the iron, the belt or a pot. It was pretty much just about anything she could get a hold of.

I was raised in the church. Going to church on a Sunday with my grandmother was extremely gratifying. I would spend time reading my Bible, as my grandmother taught me. I also loved writing, so I had a diary or a little journal and my grandmother encouraged this habit. When I wasn't crying I was always humming or singing, and I discovered that music was my escape. Singing, reading my Bible and writing were outlets that aided me through the abuse from my mother. I sang in the choir, and I had such a powerful voice that even my pastor would comment on it. Teaching Sunday school was another responsibility which I absolutely enjoyed because it was the ultimate escape from being home. Being around other people was therapeutic. At church, I felt like a normal kid especially because I didn't feel like I had a learning disability.

During that time, my grandmother was the best human being in the world to me. She knew about my disability, but she also knew that it was something that hurt me so she never highlighted the fact. Instead, she would have heart to heart conversations with me and constantly reminded me by saying, "I want you to know that you are blessed, you are special.

There is nothing wrong with you." She would say, "Who cares if you need extra time to understand certain things?" She is responsible for moulding me and keeping me in the know about anything I was unaware of. My grandmother sat with me and took the time to encourage me to push through any obstacle I faced in life. "Christine, push through it, you can do it." She would often drill me. The term mentor adequately describes her role in my life because she was more than my grandmother; she was the only person who really cared.

My troubles were far from over, because attending public school with a learning disability was like a daily tooth extraction. The psychological impact was disconcerting to say the least, but what really took its toll on me, was life during Middle School. At that point, I experienced puberty. Not only were my physical changes taking place but I started developing more emotions. Worst of all, I had an anger problem. It was so overwhelming it gave me an abnormal feeling. I would chide myself internally as to why my brothers and sister got the opportunity to experience certain things which I did not. How could they do certain things without being told whilst I sat there and pondered? In my mind I'd be like okay, "So what did you really say?" "What did you really want me to do again?" It got to the point where I no longer felt like I belonged to the family. Then, on top of all those troubles, I was the lightest one in the family.

In the Caribbean the phrase "High Colour" means a person of a lighter skin complexion. My mom would use that phrase in a negative way to say that I wasn't worth anything. Additionally, she would make comparisons between my sister and me saying that one day I would be working for my sister. All these degrading comments were ingrained in my subconscious and caused me to start believing these lies about myself. This stumped my growth in many ways, and I am still uprooting the final vines of a poisoned emotional tree.

I continued to grow into my adult life quietly doubting everything I did and second guessing my every move. It could be the smallest thing. If I was going to a job interview I would automatically tell myself that I wasn't going to be successful. When I was about to become a parent, I told myself that I would be no good at it, mostly because I feared I would become my mother. I thought about all the things I was told I couldn't do or couldn't achieve, and how I would not be able to guide my child if I lacked the skills required for motherhood. This "Doubtful Thomas" shadow that was cast over me prevented me from forming meaningful relationships with others. I didn't want that. It led me to become anti-social because I was locked up in the house frequently. Whenever I did get a break to go out into the real world, I didn't know how to relate to my peers; it was as if everything was brand new to me. Having a conversation was foreign to me, as well as a simple introduction like "Hey, my name is Christine." I no longer knew how to do that.

Many things were hard for me to do. Instead of my mom taking the time to guide me, she just made it all about me being a broken or damaged person.

CHAPTER 2

ICE BATH

When I was growing up my ambition was to become a doctor. Because of this aspiration, I made sure to take the required courses when I got to High School. Maybe there were more courses I should have taken, but not much was expected of me because of the semantics of the learning disability. Essentially, they tried to make school more of a breeze for me. My classes were smaller and I completed only one or two subjects at my own pace. So I ended up doing English and Geography.

Throughout Middle School there were teachers who knew about my situation, and I was grateful for them because they helped me significantly. They would get me the additional books that I needed and they would spend extra time with me whenever I had to prepare for exams or tests. They made it a more fun experience, so I was not afraid to use my hands or count with objects. The teacher would do certain things to build my memory when it came to math, and she got every tool you could think of to build my math skills. She got me books, supplies, and she would sit there and read the lessons repeatedly. She introduced me to computer programs that I could do at home because she knew a little bit about my family dynamics when it came to my mother. I told her certain things so she would give me some extra time. If school was over by 3:15 pm, I would stay there until 4:30 pm or when she was leaving to go home. She would see me on my way out and make sure I was okay. This continued and became my escape route.

If that was not happening after school I would be singing. I also loved to read as a child, so if it wasn't singing or reading, then it would be writing or something else. At home, I had to learn how to do multiplication and I had to teach myself how to memorize the 1 to 10 charts. I would get beatings for whatever I didn't know, and I would have to go back and redo what I missed the first time to make sure I got it the next time.

I remember I had a principal who realized that I had a punctuality problem. He made it fun for me to come to school by establishing a coupon system. As long as I was on time, the coupons afforded me a hot meal for breakfast or lunch. He bought my favourite cereals and a lot of cool stuff that I liked to eat. Even though I had shit to deal with the night before, whenever I came to school there was peace. The principal would bring me into the office and express his concern about the challenging nights I was having. With just one look at my face he would ask, "How do you want to start your day?" "Do you want this or do you want that?" It made things interesting for me. I could forget about what I had to deal with at home and just focus on school. He only put that Breakfast and Lunch Program in place because of me. The school never had any such program before. However when he heard certain things about my family dynamics, and when he saw me come to school hungry for whatever reason, he went the extra mile. As the principal he provided me with a grocery allowance to buy things that I liked to eat. He was just my principal. He left the school when I graduated and I never saw him again.

Middle School was rough with puberty just kicking in. To add insult to injury, I was a little later than everyone else. I was ashamed of my body because it did not grow as fast as every other girl in my class who was flourishing. I used to get bullied and picked on and I didn't really know how to defend myself. A lot of people in school would kick, push, and call me names. Eventually, I got into a couple of fights. It would seem as if I took on more of the nerd persona. However, I loved sports like track and volleyball, oh and yes, I loved entertainment, drama and music.

I used to get a lot of awards in school such as the Future Ace Awards and Student of the Month. Eventually I led the Bully System and did Safety Patrol with the younger kids in my school. I was responsible for walking them to school and for walking them across the street. Acting was another fun hobby I loved. I was always participating in the play, the announcements, musical theatre, you name it. I kept myself busy because of what I was going through at home. School was my escape and when I was there, I just lived in the moment. I tried out for the Volleyball and Track Teams, and drama and music activities. I auditioned for everything in order to maintain some type of focus.

The Future Ace Award required the teachers to select a student with whom they worked one on one and who displayed certain qualities. I was always smiling, friendly and helpful to my teachers. Often, I would offer to help them with their extra tasks like photocopying or making announcements. I never expected anything in return, but I guess it stood out to them and they selected me to receive these awards.

I remember being in Middle School. I called myself a bird in a cage because all I really did was pick up after other kids. I loved being outside and if she gave me the chance to go outside, I would jump at it. There was this one time I was outside playing a game called 'Manhunt' with the kids in the neighbourhood. My mom called me and told me to come inside. I responded by saying I would be there in a minute. I wanted so badly to enjoy the company and finish the game, and so like any other kid, I continued playing. This must have pissed my mom off so she decided to come outside, drag me by my hair- kicking and screaming, and drag me up the stairs. When she told me to come inside, she also told me to take a shower. I told her I wasn't ready and that I wanted to finish the game so she made sure to set the bath way before. Little did I know that I was in for a rude awakening, because the bath that she set was a cold water bath. She threw me in the tub with the cold water.

There were ice cubes in this bath and this is where insult meets injury. My mother called each and every person in the neighbourhood to watch me bathe. I remember screaming, crying, and pleading with this crazy woman. I was asking her to stop and she was just jeering and telling everybody to look at me not wanting to bathe. She called me nasty as people stood, watched and took pictures and videos. She forced the whole ordeal to continue as I felt shamed and humiliated.

My mother grabbed the soap and said, "Soap up yourself, clean yourself." I had to do all of that right in front of everybody. They laughed as I was degraded and my privacy invaded. I felt so violated. I had to live in this neighbourhood, go to school in this neighbourhood, and pass by these people daily after this torturous ordeal. At that point I wanted to die; I didn't want to live anymore. There was no point in living because whatever image I had as a child was already destroyed in the neighbourhood. How am I supposed to walk to school? The worst thing happened while I walked to school. Everyone whispered and gossiped. The jokes hurled, "Hey did you see the video of Christine bathing in the bathtub and how her…" it was just horrifying.

I didn't really have a close friend to confide in and with whom I would share my situation at home. I didn't really get close to people. My daily social life consisted of being in and out of fights. So I was either fighting someone, or starting something and it was just my way of lashing out because of bottled up anger. I did not care if I got into trouble because what could be worse than what my mom did to me at home? If she was not hitting me with a belt, she was calling me all these names. So what is a school suspension or fighting a girl really gonna do to me?

I never cared about having friends. Everybody that I made friends with turned out to be one of her friends or one of her enemies. It was easy for me to become enraged- just say the wrong thing and I would go off. But there was this one neighbourhood friend. She was around for only a short time because I was not allowed to do much with her. Being inside so much was not helping my new friendship. Whenever she would want to ride bikes and she asked my mom for permission she would receive a flat out no in response. I did not have many people in Middle School that I was close to; I was more figuring out who I was, why certain things were happening to me and what was next.

I may not have had a handful of friends in Middle School but I did have a few. Then there were always those who, out of jealousy, tried to see how far they could push me. As a result, there were a couple fights I had in Middle School and a couple of fights in High School. I was just battling emotions. One minute I would be fine and then someone would say something and I would be out of my entire element. It could be the most simple thing that I would hear a student say, and I would instantly become enraged.

I just kept fighting. Most of the time people would just pick on me and I would just start fighting. I remember I fought this girl in school because she called me out and I heard she was telling people in the school that I was promiscuous. I wasn't anything like that and I just remember my whole skin went cold. I felt fire in my stomach that I had never really felt before. I had rage like my mother and my father, but this was magnified anger. I went looking for her at the usual hang out - a restaurant spot. I asked everyone who knew her if they saw her. Then I found her and I got back to school - and no doubt I whooped her ass. Everyone said the way I fought was not normal because I threw her through a glass window and walked off.

Another incident was in Middle School. I fought a girl before my graduation ceremony. Right before I was supposed to walk up and get my diploma, the fight started. I beat up a girl and then ran across the stage and collected my certificate. It was nothing but a stupid fight. Someone told me that a girl said things about me. If I had sense back then, the right thing would have been to ask her. Turned out she never said the things I was accusing her of. I was in my dress, she was in her dress, and it was bad. There was hair pulling, kicking, and throwing across the floor. I beat her up and I heard my name, so I grabbed my pin on my ponytail, put it right back in place as if it never came off, walked into the stadium across the stage and I got my diploma. Later on I found out that I got suspended for the beginning of the next school year and I had to go to summer school.

Then, I beat this girl up in school. We lived in the same neighbourhood, and whenever I saw her we would keep fighting. We'd just fight each other and it was like sparring practice. As long as we spotted each other, if she was with her brother, if I was with my sister, or if our moms were present - it would be on.

We eventually cut out the shenanigans. It is quite a funny story, me writing this book and actually meeting up with this same arch nemesis from school days. As we spoke and took a walk down memory lane, we both concurred that we were just young and dumb with nothing better to do. Most of the kids that I fought with at that time eventually mended their relationship with me, because we have now become responsible adults.

There was this guy I dated who I really thought was going to be there for me as moral support. Little did I know that while I was in counselling, recuperating and battling my demons, he hooked up with my best friend. We fought, and she ended up moving away and eventually stayed away. She tried to contact me, but things were never the same.

In High School, I wasn't really focused on what I wanted to do professionally. I craved my freedom so I started hanging out with a group of friends. That's when I was exposed to smoking. I started to smoke and started to skip class. Basically I just did what I wanted to do. By sixteen I was kicked out by my mother.

The decision to leave my mom's house and live with my grandmother was firmly made. Everything that happened was overwhelming and my mother was toxic. I didn't want to be a part of that anymore so I left to stay with my grandmother. Sadly I returned, but I just needed some time. I didn't feel like I ever really got over the abuse. I just put it behind me because I needed to move on with my life.

I was transitioning as a teenager and I was becoming an adult. It seemed I was forced to go on instead of really healing. My therapist kept telling me to get over it. Even my mother was telling me to get over it. The nerve of her. There were no progressive steps toward true healing. I did the counselling, but I didn't go far with the process. That's when

I knew my anger started showing and I didn't feel like I was ready to heal. So I ended up walking out of many sessions and not going to a lot of the programs because I wasn't ready. Over time I learned to isolate myself from everyone, because after that happened, the only person I really connected with was my grandmother, and few members of my immediate family.

I met my dad at sixteen years old. He showed up at the door during my sixteenth birthday bash that my grandmother planned for me. I was quite confused. I didn't really know who he was. He did not give much of an introduction. He just said "I'm your father." We would speak every now and then. At times he came to my school to pick me up for lunch. I didn't know much about him, so the purpose of the meet up was to get to know him. It wasn't a forced relationship- yet, somehow, at the age of sixteen I just felt like it was too late. I was already half way through the prime of my young life. Why would he want to show up all of a sudden?

He was pretty much around for about the next two years, and when I was eighteen I went to live with him. It was possible that I wanted to have the experience of living with a father-my biological one. While living with him he would watch me like a hawk. He would do things that a father wasn't supposed to do, like intruding on my telephone calls and invading my privacy. He wanted to know where I was going, what I was doing, how I was doing it and that was just too much for me. It felt like there was no room to breathe around him. I didn't really know much about him, so having him up in my face all the time wasn't something I could deal with. What's even worse is that I didn't stay there for long. I only stayed there for a year.

The new relationship went downhill fast. One night my sister came over, and even though I was planning to go to my boyfriend's house that night, she asked me to help her do some laundry. At my dad's, I knew that doing laundry was expensive unless it was at night or on the weekends. During those hours it was cheaper and didn't cost much. So I waited until night so me and my sister could go downstairs. We started doing laundry, and for some reason he woke up out of his bed in a rage. He yelled at me for using the washer and said I was being sneaky. He removed the clothes and threw them on the floor. Then, he became physically aggressive with me.

That was a line he couldn't uncross. Once he did that I blacked out. I ended up draping him by his shirt, and pushed him against the door. I looked him right in his face and let him know, "I understand that I'm your kid but you do not have the right to put your hands on me because I wouldn't blink an eye to end it all." I could hear my sister and my step mom in the background telling me, "No, Christine don't do it, he's not worth it, leave him alone!" I heard them saying this and that, but as I said, dealing with so much rage and mixed emotions as a child, I didn't really care. The way I saw it, I didn't care if you were my father. You really haven't done anything to have these privileges with me. If you were in my life and you showed me how to do certain things, I wouldn't really say anything. As it was, he was just a stranger. I understood that on paper he was my father but I didn't really know him, so I defended myself.

During the fight, I accidentally dented the washer and he went over the edge about the damage. He even wanted to call the police. He told me to leave his house and I said, "Yeah sure, no problem." I proceeded to go upstairs and packed my bags, however my sister drew my attention to the fact that it was too late at night for us to leave. So we waited until morning and then we departed. There was some stuff left behind so I returned later with my cousin and got my stuff. I never looked back in that direction. This occurred while I was eighteen or nineteen. Our relationship is now non-existent.

CHAPTER 3

ELEMENTS OF ME

My first job had to do with mentoring within my neighbourhood. I worked with Toronto Community Housing. I was responsible for creating a group for people and kids in the neighbourhood, and we had to attend meetings and speak about what we wanted in order to make the neighbourhood safer. The neighbourhoods that my mom chose to live in were always associated with gun violence. It was a fulfilling job and I continued to work there until I decided to leave- because my mother would come to my workplace and taunt me.

She embarrassed me in front of my co-workers and my boss. I remember one incident when my siblings called and asked me for money. I told them in no uncertain terms, that they were no longer my responsibility and that they should ask their mother. She may have been deeply offended, because she came to my workplace and slapped me right across my face -in front of my boss and fellow co-workers.

Then came my wrath. Enough was enough. The bible says "Honour thy Father and Mother", but she definitely provoked this child to wrath. A fight broke out between the two of us.

I have held different jobs. Currently I am a Customer Service Sales Representative and I also do counselling in my community. I am a Mental Health Worker in my spare time and I am responsible for establishing mentorships for kids that have gone through trauma- similar to what I've gone through or even worse. Sometimes we create presentations on platforms that are easily accessible to them with topics such as Family Life, Education, Health & Sexuality, and Mental Well-Being among other areas of interest and relevance. My co-workers and I put together little guides for teenagers to follow. At times I share my experiences with them, but I always let them know that they do not have to go through every experience in life.

I was molested so I implore them to watch their surroundings and not to trust everybody around them. If a family member is behaving unseemly, it is cause for concern. Yet it seems the presentation slides are never enough; they always have questions directed towards me quite often. They ask me things like, "How did you grow up?" I let them know that I had somewhat of an disadvantage growing up because of the learning disability. I don't hide the truth about any of my past from them. I share my knowledge on whatever they want to know and provide honourable service for their peace of mind. One question I always get from the kids is: "How is my life different now that I am a mother versus when I was a child?" My answer to that question is that being a mother has taught me how to have patience so that I can manage my anger. I must be that tower of strength for my child to look up to, while still being gentle and loving.

From my own experience with my mom, I have learned the importance of listening and paying attention to my child. I go beyond simply paying attention to what my child is doing. I get involved in watching the shows and movies she likes. We set aside our own one-on-one bonding time so we can create memories together. As a child, my mother didn't do that so there are only rotten memories. All I knew was that she was my mother, we lived in a house, she made food but there was no quality time. It was more like you're my mother and I'm supposed to listen to whatever you tell me to do because it is the law.

My grandma passed away three years ago. It was very hard for me to deal with. I don't feel like anybody understood me the way she understood me. When I had certain problems or decisions that I was faced with, she was always the person I would run to for help and as I tried to figure things out. The fact that I don't have her around anymore, means I can't do a lot of the things I wanted to do- like telling my story. When I was a child I told her that I wanted to write this book about my life. She basically told me, "Yes. Do it." It would help me heal. I was in the process of preparing the script, but when I lost her I just blacked out. I didn't care much about anything. We spoke about this book for years. I would want her to know that I am thankful for everything she has done, and without her I wouldn't be the woman that I am today. I would not have been able to overcome all the statistics that I overcame in my life, if not for her.

Life as a mother has been challenging because there are certain questions I have about parenting that I would like to discuss with my Mother or Grandmother. However, I don't have the opportunity to do so. I'm doing it all by myself even though my fiancé, her father, is present in our lives. I would have loved it if I had that mother-daughter relationship with my mother. When other people say their moms are there for them during pregnancy and that they can tell their moms anything, I don't know what that means because I don't have that. I don't feel like there is anything in this world that I can do to be accepted by my mother. It's just a write off. It is something that I wish I could change because I know that the negative thoughts she harboured about me in the past are unfounded.

I have overcome a number of obstacles she may have thought I would have never overcome. I did not get pregnant at sixteen years old, did not drop out of school but graduated - while still managing to make a living for myself and be a great mother to my baby girl. It is so strange but my biggest fear is becoming her. For instance, what if I exhibit traits similar to her? I fear not wanting to listen to my daughter and shutting her out because of my past experience with my mother.

I do my best as a mother but I am still growing and learning. I have come this far. My daughter is about to turn five. I find it so hard because my mom is not there and I understand that she never will be. My grandma is not here either and I would have asked her all my questions about parenting. I know my daughter and I will be close. No secrets. Everything that is important to her is important to me. No jealousy should come between us.

The colour of our skin or the type of hair we both have should never become a point of contention between us.

I read to my daughter and I tell her everyday that I love her and that I am grateful to be her mother and that I am grateful she is my daughter. I speak words of affirmation and say, "You are beautiful, you can do anything and you are strong." My mother really didn't do any of that and she didn't really say I love you.

I congratulate my daughter on anything she does, and affirm her by telling her how proud I am of her accomplishments. Even when she makes little mistakes, I know she is still growing, so I explain any timeouts that she is given and why she is getting them. I don't just send her to her room when she does something wrong. I don't lash out at her and give her the silent treatment. I talk to her. For instance I would say, "Okay you know you did this and Mommy is not happy and this is why you need a time out." So there is more of an understanding and a level of trust that extends between me and my daughter.

When I had my daughter, I didn't refuse any type of relationship with my mother or father so as not to deprive my daughter of having grandparents in her life. This was an opportunity for my mother to redeem herself as a crappy parent and succeed as a grandparent. I was confident that I had sifted the negative family stereotypes from my offspring's upbringing. All I needed to focus on was the quality of communication between my mother and my daughter.

I had to ensure my mother didn't carry the same type of vengeance she had for me towards my daughter. I would come to find out later that Mom is who she is and she will never change. I overheard her saying things to my daughter like, "You're mom's like a deadbeat, she's 'whutless', she's stupid, she has no sense." That negative energy had no place around my daughter. She doesn't need to hear that. She's a child and she should stay a child, so I just basically cut my mother off. I did not want to deal with it anymore. I tried; I excused her behaviour for a while, always censoring verbiage to protect my little girl while still giving her a real chance at knowing my mother- her grandmother and nana. However, things were not okay with her mother and her nana because I still had so much hatred for my mother, and for good reason.

She would do anything to hear from me, but she is blocked on every platform- both phone and iPad. When she can't get to me, she will try to get to one of my siblings. She'd ask my sister, "How is she? Still struggling with her life?" Her desire is to hear that I'm in need of help. In her mind, it pleases her to think that she did all this shit to me and I still ran to her for help, but that will never be the case. During the last phone conversation we had, I made it clear, "If there's ever a situation that I'm in, I prefer to walk naked and claim that I'm a mad person before I ever walk back into your house!"

I feel a lot especially considering what I've been through and having to do mentorship. There are many trigger moments that I experience. When they talk about my mother I am triggered because I don't really want to hear anything about her. I don't like talking about her because I do not like her. I will never understand what would make a mother give up on her child in the way she totally gave up on me.

I enjoy being around my daughter and spending time with her. If I was ever given the opportunity to give up on her, it wouldn't be an option- it would be impossible to even consider. There are certain things that come up in conversation like, "Tell us a little bit about what you went through as a child" or casual questions about Mother's Day or Family Day. I don't really have any of those memories. My friends would be like "You know me and my mom talk every night" or "My mom was there for my pregnancy." My mom does this or that. This lady can't relate to any of those eventualities. So I'm faced with a lot of emotion sometimes and it hurts me to my core. In my case it's not one parent, but two that messed up, which caused me to manoeuvre through the world mostly on my own. For me, I'd say it's been trial and error.

What I want people to take from my story, is that even though I faced these obstacles and challenges in my life, I never gave up. I always see a light through any situation. So whether it was me being angry or sad, I always knew that there was more to me than the situation I was experiencing.

She really didn't take responsibility for anything. Whenever I would bring up the story of the cold water treatment, she would say she never did that. She said she was the best parent to me. I would look at her and tell her she must be nuts, because unless I had two different mothers, the one she thought she was to me was not the mother I had. I don't want to mend anything with her and I don't want anything to do with her. She's done too much and it's more damage than repair. In retrospect, the things that she did growing up encouraged me to be the 'bigger person'. It helps to think about it this way just to establish some sort of resolve.

I sat down as a child and tried to understand why she did what she did; why she didn't raise me in the way that she ought to have. Every time I forgave her she would do something worse. I would often wonder how she had so much time on her hands to walk around the neighbourhood and spread bad rumours about me. She would tell my brothers and sister that I'm satan's spawn. She would say I'm not of her and that she wished she aborted me. If I did not find my wings and exercise my freedom, she would still do things to taunt me. Before I had a child she would tell people that I was barren and that my womb was closed. Normal parents don't say things like that to their child. She would say I am never going to find a man, that I am going to end up pregnant and on drugs and that the only thing I am good for is whatever is between my legs - that is why I open them so frequently.

She allowed men to force themselves onto me, and if she was more of a mother men would have never got the chance to come near me. She was careless and yet she uses derogatory terms when speaking about me. I had a clear view of her life. I would watch her go through many relationships, so my idea of a perfect man is skewed in so many ways because she never really had one.

CHAPTER 4

TORTURE

One problem I am encountering right now is that I have to tip-toe around my whole family. Even my sister, who is really close to me, does not know I am writing this book. When people inquire about my distractions or my Zoom meetings, I just cast their attention to the fact that I do mental health work; and that I am busy preparing a mental health campaign on Zoom for the kids. By the time this book is produced, they may still not know.

My cousin was recalling incidents from my past that eluded my memory. As we spoke, she prodded, "You do realize that because of your mom's physical, emotional and verbal abuse, you have PTSD?" I kept going back and forth with her and I was like "I don't have PTSD." She was like "Yes, the fact that you keep repeating something you cannot let go of indicates you are traumatized by it." My cousin went on to give me little fillers for the things that I could not recall. I didn't even remember all of those things. She went on to describe the things I had to do like waking up early to cook and clean. I started to remember as she continued to speak. Her visits to our home were frequent so she experienced how my mom used to lock me in the house from Monday to Friday and I had to clean the house. There were times she said I would go hungry because my mom would lock the cupboards with all the food. On another occasion my mom came up to me from behind me and hit me with a pot in my head. My cousin recounted that as I fell to the floor, she came into the kitchen after my mom walked off, asked me if I was okay and checked to see if I was bleeding.

Sometimes when we recount a story we forget that there were other people involved, people who saw the trauma I went through with my mother. The story is not always just mine to tell. When other people can speak about incidents in your life, that is a whole other realm of horror.

I told her I was going to make my life into a movie and that I would sign my name on papers and be famous. By now she should be reading this book- and she will be in awe about how the future has unfolded-and how the words that I spoke are coming to pass.

I want my readers to know that I became all these things because of all the obstacles I went through in my life. This is how I became a mother. Fight. That is what I did. I had to fight and persevere through all the terror that rained down on my childhood. I remained strong and made something of myself. The full goal has not yet been accomplished but it is enough for my daughter to see and be proud of. I always saw the light at the end of the tunnel. I don't know if that was because of my grandmother. She instilled that habit in me- and she always said that with everything you go through in life, if it is written, it can also be unwritten.

At the age of sixteen years old, I went to live with my aunt after living with my grandmother. I stayed once at my pastor's house and some nights I slept in the hallway-yes in the stairwell of our apartment. This happened because my mom would kick me out and I would have nowhere to go. At times I would be at a friend's for just a little bit. I couldn't stay there for long because many people did not want to provoke my mom.

The whole neighbourhood already knew who she was, so some nights I slept in the hallway, in the stairwell or by the door. In the morning, I would only have enough time to sneak inside and change my clothes to go to school. I slept outside for a good couple of days, until a friend who saw the situation repeatedly took me into their house. Her mom was a nurse or Personal Support Worker (PSW) who worked at night, so she would sneak me in when her mom left. By morning, it would be time for school, and her mom would never know I was there. On occasion I could freshen up at her house, and at other times I would freshen up in the school bathroom-because sometimes I wasn't able to enter my house at all.

Back at my house, my mom warned my brothers and sister not to open the door for me. So I threw rocks at my sister's room, which was my room as well, so she could open the door. She would say "I can't, mom said no or she's gonna beat me and take away my stuff." They were kids you know, they couldn't really do much.

There were times I didn't have sanitary napkins for my menstrual cycle. Many times when I slept in the hallway, I was on my period. I would be in the middle of fighting or arguing, and I would be like "Oh my God, my thing is coming up!" By the time I got to the door, it was locked, the alarm code was activated and my mom went to bed. She would literally hear me begging at the door saying, "All I want is a tampon, can I get a pad?" And she would say, "No, no, stay out there tonight and bear hard life." My only other option was to go to the dollar store, and buy little wet naps to have what my grandma used to call "quick bath".

After that incident and just before I started my second year of High School, I moved out to live with my grandmother. I was about to start Grade Ten and I was fifteen . I didn't stay with my grandmother permanently, but for the time I was there, I had to switch schools. My first High School was in the Jane and Finch area. I finished my remaining year at that school while I lived with my grandmother. Then I got kicked out because of the fight, so I went to a different school and I moved back in with my mother. She sent for me and my Grandma begged me to stay connected with the family. So I went back.

An incident happened when I was sixteen and that was the final straw. My mother asked me to do something and I basically told her "No." My younger brother got involved and I got so angry. Although I told him to stay out of it, he just kept pushing and poking at me because that is what my mom would do when she wanted to start ramblings between me and my siblings. She would set them on me. On that day, in the midst of the conversation, I told my brother, "Say another word and I'll bust your face!" My mom immediately took that, ran with it and called the cops on me. She told them that she no longer wanted me in her house.

The cops gave me two options: I could either call someone to come and get me or I could spend my night in a shelter. Based on what I knew from friends who had been in shelters and what they taught me in school, I did not want to go to a shelter. So I decided to call my aunt. As soon as I told her my mom was kicking me out and I had nowhere to go, she said, "I'll be there in ten minutes." She told me to grab all my stuff and meet her outside. I didn't even stay outside the apartment after the cops left. Instead, I waited at the park with all my belongings on a bench until my aunt got there.

Life with my aunt was way better. She taught me what family dynamics really were. She taught me what it meant to have a family, and even though she was my aunt, she treated me more like a daughter. At her house I had responsibilities, but my main job was to go to school. She told me "Even if you don't get a job, I need you to graduate." So that was my goal.

The school I attended while living with her was rough. The type of schools that I had to go to were called Special Schools. They were like an alternative school. Even though I had a learning disability, I did not want to go to that school. This involved being picked up by a school bus when I was sixteen going on seventeen, and I was tall so taking the bus was definitely a problem. When it arrived, I would hide in the bushes and then have the door open for a while until I was sure no one was looking. Then I dashed toward the bus, with my head held down.

This school had kids with special needs and disabilities. There were kids like me but they had more mental disabilities. They mixed me with everybody- physical, mental and emotional. The good thing is that I made a couple of friends from there that I keep in touch with to this day. I also graduated. I was supposed to graduate at nineteen but I didn't graduate until the following year. I went to High School, but I never went to college.

My aunt is the person who really showed me the ropes and the rules of being a woman and she taught me how to take care of myself. She taught me how to cope with life. She knew all about the problems I had with my mom and all the obstacles I faced. She always told me that even though my life was rough, that that was not what my life was all about. With every obstacle I faced, she explained this is you but it is not of you. She told me to look at it as if it were a time or a moment. It had come to pass. When it passes over you will welcome something else. Ever since then, I have stopped blaming myself and wishing I was different or normal. I got to a place of self-acceptance; this is who I am so it's either you take me or leave me.

My aunt gave me travel experience. I never knew anything about travel so whilst living with her I travelled with her family often. We went to the United States and we went to Jamaica for vacation. I stayed with her family in Jamaica for a day, and then we would do our own site seeing. We went on excursions, rented a guest house, and I became exposed to the party scene. It was so much fun. For a few parties I lived life a little, which was a contrast to always being caged. I called myself a 'bird in a cage' because I never knew certain things.

We went to Montego Bay and Mandeville. I even got to be in a couple video shoots and music videos. I met a lot of artists. It was fun living with her. My aunt was in school and she was also a mom to her three kids and me. It was against the Building Code Rules to take me in because of the capacity breach, but she loved me dearly and made the room for me anyway. Her kids were younger than I was; two girls and one boy. We were very close.

To this day, my aunt can't believe the things that my mother did to me. One time my aunt wanted to call her and destroy her when she heard my mom was telling people I couldn't have kids and I was sick in a way. I told my aunt to just leave it alone. I begged her actually because I knew what my Aunt would do.

She's actually my mother's really close friend from long ago and is more of a aunt to all of my mother's children. She took more of a liking to me growing up because she saw what I went through. She has been my escape route for years. Whenever I used to leave my mom's house because of the abuse, I went to her house and I stayed there for weeks or months at a time. As a kid, I told her I wanted to live with her. My aunt would have done the paperwork, but my mom would never agree. Eventually at sixteen years old, that happened. No paperwork was necessary to keep me at that age. It was my own choice to make.

I only went around my mom's house when I had to go to work. Since I used to work for Toronto Community Housing that's the only time I was ever in that neighbourhood or close to my mother. When I went to work my aunt would call me and say, "Did you get to work?" "Yes." "Did you get back from work okay?" "Yes." There was no communication between me and my mom. My aunt even asked me about my mom's wedding. "Do you want me to drop you there?" I told her, "No, I don't want to go." Despite everything my mom did to me, my aunt always allowed me to make my own decisions. She would reassure me and say it was fine if I wanted to visit and speak with her because, after all, she was my Mom. I would tell her, "No, I don't want to talk to her. Leave me alone. Stop bringing her up. I want to block her out and heal."

I just let it pass and she never judged me for my decision. She would say, "I'm not blaming you if you don't want to talk to her, I understand. I get that a lot of things she does to you are inhumane." My aunt taught me core family values because she didn't just take me in, she treated me the way a mother would treat her own child. I was family. I never missed out on a portrait or a family photo or a trip. I was included. I wasn't left out the way my mom would treat me. So on Mother's Day, I would give my aunt and my grandmother all the props. Those are the two females who were the mother figures in my life.

My sister, on the other hand, will buy my mom her gifts. Until last year I was still buying her gifts as well. Not just because she was a mother, but because I actually wanted to do these things for her. She didn't even call and say thank you in return. When I started working, my first pay check went towards helping her out. Despite everything she has done, I still used to stretch my hand further than I should have.

As a young adult, I aspired to be a Child Support Worker. To this day I still want to do this, and it is a work in progress. I had to start somewhere, so I started volunteering at Community Centres and I got involved with the youth. I went into programs that prepared students for college and I did work as an Aesthetician. I also worked at Shoppers Drug Mart, and in a Beauty Supply store, which was something I wanted to do as a young person. I also worked in retail in different positions.

My mom was still taunting me at every turn and spreading rumours about me. She was telling people I was a whore and that I wouldn't make anything of myself. She basically spun the story to her narrative. She never told people what really happened the night she kicked me out, so many people would ask "Why would you do that to your brother and to your mother?" They did not know the truth about how she was the person in the background, stringing her children like puppets, severely abusing me and destroying my life. She deceived other people by poisoning their opinions of me with lies. She would spread rumours that I was pregnant. On another occasion she would say that I was barren, could never have children and that there was something wrong with me.

As if that were not enough, she turned my siblings against me- because for a long time when I was living with my aunt, I didn't really have anything to do with them. Honestly, it made me feel some type of way but I had to go through it all to become the person I am today. So once they cut me off, I cut myself off from the family. The only person I communicated with was my grandmother and she would update me on current events. She informed me that my mom was getting married and asked if I wanted to attend. I told her "No!" Some relatives pleaded with me to reconcile with her, but I knew who she was and that nothing would change.

A perfect example is when I found out my mother had a relationship with my ex-boyfriend. She breeds a certain quantity of hatred and vengeance for me, so everything she did was an attempt to hurt me. There were lies, there were rumours, but that whole ex-boyfriend scenario was top tier evil. Imagine your mother getting involved with whom you were once intimately engaged. It broke me. It doesn't even make me want to have a relationship with her. How can a mother consciously do something like that to her own child?

That put me in a deep depression. Of course I did not care for this man who was from my past relationship. I walked out on it, but it was the principle of it all. When confronted, he said he didn't know, but that was a lie because I saw the messages between them. The first thing she said to him was her name and that she was Christine's mother. He just denied it, said he didn't know and finally apologized. Then he tried to get me to take him back. I cut him off. Maybe they wanted to qualify for Jerry Springer or Maury but I was not into that.

Meanwhile my mother denied everything though I had the proof. She tried to say it wasn't anyone I cared for so what was the big deal? The fact that she went to the extent of trying to fill a void with someone that I already had a relationship with-a sexual relationship at that-says a lot about who she truly is. Why would you want any part of that? I told her that I don't try to be with any of her past partners just to spite her. That's nasty. At the end of the day, I know the truth about what happened.

With my daughter's paternal grandfather, my heart aches because I don't know what anyone is capable of doing. I don't want her to experience what I experienced, so I am very careful. I am also very strategic about who is around her and I watch every little move. Even with her own father-I really don't care. I have a guard up and I talk to him about how I feel.

That is the reason I need to write this book. I need all these feelings to be released. I need to put it all in this book, and put it out there so I can just live my life instead of living in doubt or fear, and having these things in my mind. What if somebody tries to hurt my child? What would happen? I'm tired of feeling like this. I'm tired of the what ifs and walking on eggshells with people. I want to meet people and be around them free of any fear- not just for my daughter but for my life.

Now I am so closed off and so disconnected. A person would be lucky if they even get a peep of who I am inside. I cut people off easily. As long as it doesn't work for me, I don't have time for it. When I cut it off, I cut off everything- I cut off you and I cut off the relationship with my daughter because I don't want there to be a return door. I do not create any opportunity for you to come back into my life. I just don't have time.

Because of what I went through, I have the tools and the safety kit. I know what to do and no one will come close to my daughter at all- I don't care who it is. I teach her all the time; if anybody comes close to you, know that is your personal space. No one is supposed to touch your private parts. Do not just look to call the cops. The first person you come to is me. As your mother, you tell me, you tell your father, and then we will handle it. I let her know everything; there is no baby talk, everything is straight out of the book. No one should touch you where they are not supposed to be touched. I call her body parts individually, and say "your vagina, that is a no, no". You let me know.

In my case, imagine being a kid describing what happened to you at the hands of your abuser. I was just a kid and I felt like I didn't have the knowledge. No one told me that a man is not supposed to touch your vagina, or that a man is not supposed to touch your chest or that a man is not supposed to touch you at all. I was taken advantage of. I was never cautioned and told that if your father or somebody hugs you, they're not supposed to embrace you in an unusual way. I thought those things were acceptable growing up. I was never really taught that it was wrong. I never received the warning signals.

I have to share my story because I am tired of all these feelings on my chest and I need to let them go. I don't want to sit and anticipate whether something will happen. I just take heart in knowing that what I went through will never happen to my daughter. Regardless of what the circumstances are in her life, I will always be there for her. She will never feel the way I felt. I felt abandoned, alone, confused, unloved and I felt like I was being punished.

CHAPTER 5

STOLEN IDENTITY

The first time I was molested I was nine years old. I was a baby. She would call different men to come to the house. Some of these men were her friends or were friends of a friend. These parties had alcohol and people would be smoking. My room was upstairs, and I would always sit on the stairs and just watch what was going on because I was curious. Why were we sent to bed early and why were we rushed to finish eating dinner? I needed to know why she just wanted us out of her way.

I would eventually go to bed and there was this one particular man who would always ask to use the bathroom. Instead of going to the bathroom, he would sneak into my room and proceed to touch me all over my body. I knew that was not the way a man was supposed to be touching a little girl but I was in shock and confused while this demon pervert whispered in my ear that I shouldn't tell anyone because that was our secret.

My mother never had the sense to follow the man upstairs and make sure he only used the bathroom. A lot of things that happened to me happened on her watch. My mom did not have the conversations with me that she should have had with me. For example, what do you do if a man touches you inappropriately? How do you raise an alarm? There was more fear of my mom than being open with her. Because for one, she wasn't going to believe me, and what was she really going to do? In my eyes, she wasn't a safe haven.

One rule in my house is that *no one is allowed to go past my daughter's room,* and even if you go past my daughter's room, I am behind you like a hawk. My mom has denied responsibility for the assault and said *I had always wanted it, and that I've always asked for it. She keeps saying that she did what she felt she had to do as a parent.* I don't know what she is talking about because it didn't really do anything for me. It messed me up. It messed up just about everything about me. My learning disability, my anger, and being touched as a child three times began to add up. It didn't really do anything for me. When I would try to talk to her about it, she would not want to talk about it. She asks me what I want her to do about it now. "You're a grown woman", she would say. As if that should negate the abuse. All she did was shove things under a rug.

My first year of Middle School I was molested by a family member. That, combined with the learning disability was devastating.

I remember there was a time when my mother left for the day. She told us to call her if we needed anything and that we were going to be by ourselves. I got this strange call from her, and it sounded like there was partying in the background. She laughed and sounded like she was drinking. She told me that a cousin was coming by to bring us stuff for school the next day. Apparently she forgot that we had school in the morning. We had nothing in the house for sandwiches and we had no snacks for lunch. So that cousin was coming from wherever he was to drop off the food. But instead of just dropping off the food, he ended up staying.

I was in the basement and he asked me what I was doing. I used to love watching Fear Factor. So I remember I was watching that and he came and sat on the couch beside me. I was so into the show, and then all of a sudden, I started to feel his hands creeping up on my body, trying to grope me.

He tried to kiss me on my neck. I looked at him and I was

like, "What are you doing?" and he goes, "Oh, nobody has to know this can be our secret." I told him that he was my older cousin and that what he was doing was wrong. He said, "No one will know. You're growing up to be prime. So this is the next step you have to take to go into your womanhood." I was like "No!" He was still trying to force himself on me and that's when I kicked him. I used both my legs and kicked him off. He flew into the furnace of the basement and started cussing.

"You're a little bitch! You should just sit there and listen when a grown man is talking to you!" I said, "You're my older cousin, I'm like a baby to you. Why are you doing this?" He continued, "No one will know. You gotta just keep your mouth shut and just watch and just let me do what I'm doing." I remember fighting him and scratching his face. I was like, "Leave me alone!"

Somehow I managed to escape so I ran upstairs to my room and hid under my bed. While I hid under my bed, it took him a while to come up the stairs because I think I wounded him. When he came upstairs he started calling my name. "Where are you?" "All I wanna do is just play and you can play whatever game you want to play. I just want you to play by my rules." Something like that. So I covered my mouth so that he didn't hear me breathing. Then he went for my younger sister because she was in bed. She was sleeping on the bed, but I was under it, hiding.

Afterwards I received knowledge that my mom knew his whole M.O. She allowed this person in our house knowing that he was accused of doing the same thing to other children. Now he wanted to continue the pattern with her own children, and I didn't understand. He even used to stay with us sometimes and tried to fondle me under the table. When I tried to tell my mom, she basically told me that I was lying. She would say I just want attention, I just want to be grown and she would ask me what I did to make him think of me in that way. I remember bursting into tears. "There's nothing I did."I'm a kid." "You're a liar!" she said. She called me a bitch and accused me of always trying to dress scandalously in front of men or when she had male company around.

After a proper cussing, I got grounded. I was confused. I'm the one that's being sexually abused and now I'm being grounded? It sent me into a dark place because it had me really thinking, did I do something? I was so confused. I was violated to the point where I was rendered partially mute. I didn't want to do the things that my mom would ask me to do like going to the store. And, I definitely didn't want to be in the presence of men.

I started to go through a change. I didn't really want to be seen and hence I adopted the "Tom Boy" persona. As long as there was company at my house, like when extended family made visits, I would ensure my body was fully clad. I would wear baggy shorts and a T-shirt. Hair would be straight and straight back. You could find me outside with the guys, chilling on the block. I wouldn't speak unless I needed to be heard.

When that happened, I was exposed to the whole court system. The police would invade my life and my space. They would come to my school and pick me up to attend certain programs. They said it was necessary for me to heal. Those programs didn't help me heal because it wasn't the right time. Instead of healing, I started to unleash an enormous amount of rage, and my anger, like true anger, came out because I was dealing with a learning disability. I was dealing with all that in addition to being violated in my home at a young age. I wasn't even a teenager.

One of these incidents just went away with a hush. The second incident with the family member went before the courts. The police got involved and I was put into many programs.

We did not win the case because they said there was no semen found in me, and therefore it was hard to prove what happened. That so-called "relative" had people on his side. They defended him and said, "He is not this person", "He could never do this" and that he had kids of his own. None of that mattered. I know what happened and I spoke my truth.

It was so hard because I didn't really get to tell her what really happened. It was my grandmother's husband who was supposed to be my grandfather. I lived with her but that is the reason I went back home. So I tried to reconcile with my mom and give her a chance; it was the better of the two evils. When I was at my grandma's this man would sneak into my room. He would sit on my bed, touch my leg, watch me come out of the shower, and make sexual comments. I just felt gross and uncomfortable. I really wanted to stay with my grandmother but I could not endure his perverted ways. It made me sick and it hurts to this day, because I didn't really get to go in depth with my grandmother about the whole thing. Now that she is no longer here, there is nothing I can say or do. Since she passed away, I have no connections or ways of finding this man to ensure he faces the punishment he deserves. All I have is my story, my side versus his.

I also know I was not the only one he molested. I have another cousin whom certain family members know about. That is another reason why I separate myself from them. They know about it and instead of doing something, they just brush it off. He went to jail, he had a court order against him, but they bailed him out and it just went away. That's not a punishment. You basically tell the person that they can get away with it and do it again. How does something like that just go away?

My grandmother is very dear to my heart. When she found out about it, it kind of drove a wedge between us. She distanced herself from me because she didn't hear it from me. She called and asked why I didn't tell her, and my answer to her was, "You've been with this man for almost twenty-five years. How am I supposed to tell you as your granddaughter that your husband of twenty-five years is a pervert or a predator?" She was like "I know it was hard, but you should have said something to me." It was hard. I didn't want to add that to everything that was bottled up inside of me and weighed heavily on my chest. It was too much.

It was one incident after another and I did not have any peace. So my way of dealing with things was to hide, shut people out and let people figure it out for themselves. I may have left little bits and pieces like a puzzle for them to figure it out- if they cared enough about what I was going through. That situation hurts to this day. I wish I had the opportunity to spend time with her, so that I can tell her about everything that I went through while living in her house. He would just walk into the shower when I was in there and make comments about my body. I would find him on porn sites masturbating. One night I woke up, and he was masturbating at my door. That creep turned me away from living with her. Before leaving, I just told her I wanted to give my mom another try, which was of course, a lie. I just couldn't tell her what was really going on.

I was just starting school and figuring out what it meant to have friends and hang out and stuff. Then, I was robbed of that. When I went to certain therapy sessions they would tell me to think back to the incident. That wouldn't work because I was trying to forget. I was a child and I didn't want to remember my abuse. One night, when it happened, I remember trying to take my life. I had a razor in my hand as I sat in the bathroom, on top of the toilet and I just couldn't grasp what happened to me. Imagine telling your own mother and she refuses to believe that someone hurt you. It was more than I could bear.

My grandmother believed me and she tried to bridge the conversation between me and my mom. There was no explanation for her disbelief. My mom's get out of jail card would be to make up lies and say that I'm a known liar. She told my grandmother that I dressed provocatively in the house and that I wanted it to happen to me. My mother blamed me for the abuse that I went through.

I felt worthless. Even if as a child I was inappropriately dressed in her view, it was my home and where I lived in the care of my mother. This took place in a space which should have been my safe haven. The fact that it happened in my house and was done by a family member, made me feel worthless. It made me wonder what it meant to be a woman. *Was I supposed to just accept this? Was this okay?* Those were questions swirling around in my mind. The confusion that ensued caused me to believe that my mother was right about me wanting these events to happen to me. So I started to wonder what I did to make this man look at me the way he did, and what made him feel that way towards me. I went through a heap of emotions. I ended up cutting open my thigh.

I tried to suffocate myself one time because of the trouble that my brothers and sister caused while in my care. I was the eldest. I was responsible for it, and it was not even the trouble they caused, but more so the embarrassment. My brothers, my sister and I think my cousins were there. My mom came home and started complaining about the dirty dishes and the floor not being clean. "What have you done all day?" she yelled. Trying to explain was useless. It was hard because I had to watch my brothers, sister and my cousin all day, making sure everyone was okay. She did not care; she walked up to me and slapped me in my face in front of all the other kids. She continued yelling, "Get in the kitchen and start washing the dishes!" I stumbled off crying, tears rolling down my face as I washed the dishes. No one cared for me. What did I ever do in life to deserve this kind of treatment from my mother?

That night when they were all going to sleep, I had a conversation with her and I told her I was going to kill myself. I basically went through the entire plan. I took the pillow and I tried to suffocate myself. I held it down over my face with as much weight as I could, so I could take that last breath. They basically laughed at me the whole time because they thought it was so dumb for me to attempt something like that- because in their minds, it was not going to solve the problem.

I realized that my cousin cared for me; my sister on the other hand was in her own world. She was like a diva. So if it didn't fit in her schedule, she didn't really care. If it didn't have anything to do with her, she wouldn't care. I thought to myself, at the end of the day she was still quite young and still figuring herself out. My cousin on the other hand, was not close in age, but we were old enough to talk. She was basically telling me that taking my own life would not be worth it.

Although we were kids the conversation took another turn. My cousin reminded me that there was much to live for, and to look forward to -especially school and prom. She said, "What about you getting married or having children, do you really wanna miss out on all of that?" Little things like that kind of kept me grounded and I started to see a bit more clearly. My grandmother always told me to read my bible and journal, which helped me get back on track. It is also the reason why I have the strength and the capacity to write this book.

The thing is that my abuser is my mother and my father. All these other things that happened to me were bad, but nothing hurts more than the hurt from my parents. They were responsible for protecting me from all these things. These things should never have happened to me. They did not have the grit that real parents have and what I have with my daughter.

I'm so scared, so protective, so grounded, so loving, and so nurturing with my child. If they had an ounce of that with me, then I would probably be further ahead in life. I'm not saying anything they did stopped me, because it did not. But it was a huge hindrance. The trauma I went through hindered the process of going to college.

I am a mother striving to set an example for my daughter. It pains me that there are people older than me who have graduated and fulfilled their career aspirations. Now I feel as though I am running out of time. I remind myself that the sky is the limit and that I will keep reaching until I touch the sky. I was always afraid to come out of my comfort zone, but now I am living my best life.

When I finally visited her in the hospital for the last time, I cried out to her and told her that I was sorry. I was sorry for not coming around and I was sorry for staying away. My counsellor once told me that letting go meant being at peace. She probably didn't speak to let me know she forgave me, but after she let go, and while she was going in peace, she heard me pouring out everything I had to say to her. I just know in my heart that she is at peace.

I didn't go in depth, I just told her "Whatever we went through, I need you to know I love you, I need you to be here for me and my daughter." "I want her to grow up to see you." Then my cousin said whatever she had to say to her. She just let go and that was that. She was on an oxygen machine and it started to go really fast. She kept going and going then the nurse came in and told us visiting hours were over. I left the hospital at 5pm, and at around 8 or 9 I got home and began to bathe my daughter. For some strange reason, my daughter would not come out of the bath until I acknowledged that call.

I missed the first phone call which was from my mom; I didn't answer her call. Then my uncle called, but I didn't get to answer, so I returned his call. That is when he told me the news of my grandmother's passing. I didn't believe him and he said "Okay well then if you don't believe me Facetime your mother." So I did and she said: "See it deh, yuh Granny dead!" She switched the cameras showing the lifeless body of my grandmother lying in the hospital bed.

I only just started my journey as a mother. Her husband was nowhere to be found. He was just talking through her phone like a ghost and he knew he couldn't come around. Because of the person that I am, there was no way in hell he could stay in that hospital room beside her bed with me, and watch tears being shed for my grandmother- all while sitting there like nothing happened. He didn't come to the hospital and he definitely didn't come to the funeral. I am glad it turned out like that, because if he was at that funeral or if he was at the hospital, I swear to you I'd be in jail. He distorted the image of a grandfather and turned it into something ugly.

I feel like when most people have affected a child, they need to accept the fact they hurt that child. It makes no sense when people are in denial and say, "No, I didn't do this to you" or "You're a liar." It's especially traumatizing when you know what happened and the person that hurt you just sits there unaware of the damage caused. They say things like, "What are you talking about?" "I never touched you." "I never tried to have sex with you."

I don't understand how paedophiles, child molesters and

even rapists, tell themselves, "Yeah, I did not do this." "I didn't hurt that person."

I felt like that was what discouraged me from writing this years ago. Because who was really going to believe me? I was a child. I ran to the person that was supposed to protect me-my mom. She sent me on my way calling me a liar or accusing me of wanting the feeling. I don't know. How could I have kept myself quiet? I was a little girl.

She's basically said that as a kid, I was very promiscuous. And in my time, from what I remember, I was never like that. But even if you want to go with that story, a man-especially a grown man, should know about the age gap between himself and a child. I was nine when this happened. Then it happened again when I was in Middle School and a little bit before I went to High School. I was still discovering myself. I don't understand how someone could tell me, "Hey, lie down." "No, it's our little secret." That part is just sick.

It sent me into a dark place because it had me really thinking; did I do something? I was so confused.

CHAPTER 6

MY MOTHER'S CURSE

I felt as though whatever curse was invoked on her was transferred to me. I felt like my mother was the reason behind many of the things I went through. My grandma would say "If yuh cyaan ketch di hen, yuh ketch di foul." My grandma is from Jamaica and I always ask her "What does that mean?" She says "If you can't catch a chicken itself, you will catch its off-spring. So I just felt like everything my mom endured was meant for me. Whoever couldn't catch my mom, definitely caught up with me.

Growing up I heard all the stories about what my mom used to do to people and how she treated them. I have a theory that the curse of incompleteness on her, and whatever was left undone, was brought on to me. I felt like that for years, I still feel like that to this day. She was very brawling; she did not care what she did to people. That is how she dealt with you, she did not look back. I was told that she was very promiscuous. She was in a lot of drama, she was uneducated, and she did what any young parent without guidance would do. That was her.

I remember at a young age, my siblings and I had different types of punishment; mine were more extreme than the others. We used to live in this house in Malton- in an affordable housing complex. I remember the structure of the dwelling. There was a kitchen, bathroom, bedroom, an attic and there was also something called a 'Cold Room'. The Cold Room would consist of something like a boiler and a washing machine. In the summertime, it's not really a cold room because it's hot. The reason I call it the Cold Room however, is because in the winter time that is where my mom would lock me up for punishment.

The door in the room was made of wood, and although you could see shadows of people passing by the door there was no other way to see from inside. At the time it was me, my mom, my brother and sister living together in that house and it didn't matter what I did. She would lock me in there for punishment. It could be anything and for any reason. It did not even have to be related to me. For instance, she could have been in a bad relationship. My brother was a baby at the time, not a newborn, and she didn't really know a lot. I now understand that she didn't really know much about parenting, because I am now a grown woman and a mother.

She would lock me in and leave me there. All I would have on was a marina, and my underwear in the Cold Room. If it had not been for my step-sister, who was living with us at the time, I would have never come out. She would come to the door and teach me how to open the door from my side. She would fight with my mother and tell her how wicked she was because she risked her own child getting hypothermia.

I had a friend who reached out to me the other day about that incident. In my head, I was like "You remember that?" She was basically telling me that she used to think my mom was actually crazy because of the way she treated me. She continued speaking and told me "We thought she had a mental illness, and that is why she did those things. We didn't know that she was actually a sane person that just didn't think with common sense. I'm going to be real with you, we've grown up in the neighbourhood and we were like, you guys are a mental case because." I didn't really go outside, so she thought, "What parent would just keep their kid locked up inside almost all the time?"

This particular person was a childhood arch nemesis to me. She would see my other brothers and sister outside, but she never used to see me. Any time she did see me, she was one of the people I actually fought. I would lash out at her, or if she ever said anything to me, I'd be like "forget this." She never really understood what we were going through with my mother, but now that we're all grown adults and we both have kids, we have a better understanding. She basically said, "It's like your mom just didn't know how to love, like her way of showing love was not the way a mom should show love." Additionally, she told me that they used to make fun of me and tease me.

As a kid looking through my own eyes I never saw the depth of my mother's ways, and the spiralling impact it had on all our lives, until someone else who observed what was happening spoke about what they saw. My friend even spoke about the "ice bath". She confirmed a lot of things and I just thought "Wow, I am not crazy." Clearly, I was not making stuff up. I used to think that saying these things myself was one thing, and that when I said them to people I was crazy. She's like, "No girl. Your mom was, she is crazy, another level crazy."

You know as a child, adults can mistreat and abuse you, causing confusion, and making you think ill of yourself. They can make you think that you did something wrong, but when there are witnesses, even as we get older- someone to concur and confirm that all that trauma and abuse did in fact happen to you- it adds value to your life story. You don't really realize everything you have overcome until someone recites it back to you.

There were times when my mother cooked and I wouldn't get any of the food. By the time I was ready to eat she would say there was not enough, and so I wouldn't get any. My step-sister, who I really just call my sister, (because that is really who she is to me) and my brother's dad at the time, would always argue with her because of all the horrible things she used to do to me. I was just a kid; the only things that I would do were mark on the walls or spill some paint or water- regular stuff that kids do. It really didn't matter what I did, my mom didn't really have that whole quality manual. Yeah, like the whole manual. When it came to what it really took to raise a child, she just did whatever she wanted to and what she thought- as she always said, whatever benefited us. To this day, I don't really know the benefit of an ice bath as punishment for talking back.

There was even a time when my mom would send me to the store with a list, and I would miscalculate the correct change I should have received. For example if I bought something for $40 and I had $50, I may not have noticed right away if I was given $5 change instead of $10. I just didn't know at that time, and it may very well have been because of my learning disability or that I wasn't paying attention. She just liked to test me but in a way where she knew I would fail. So she would send me to the store with the list and be like, "Hey, buy this or buy that" without specifying a brand or giving any clear instructions. One time she sent me to get some sort of canned goods and she didn't specify which kind. She didn't like the one I bought so she hit me in the head with the can. My step-sister stepped in and fought with her. She threatened to call the police on my mom and told her she would take me away from her because she didn't deserve to have me.

One time, my grandma bought me a new hair salon set to play with, but instead of using the scissors from the set, I would use the real ones at home. My sister and I both had long hair and one day I called my sister upstairs in the room to give her a haircut. I think I snipped off about an inch or two from my sister's hair but in return my mom cut the majority of my hair off. She brushed my hair into a ponytail and then she just cut the whole ponytail off. It was really devastating. I was horrified. I cried and I even went to school wearing a hat, scarf or whatever I could find just to cover it. We have an older sister who used to comb our hair and she knew this was wrong. She was my safety net. When stuff happened and I wanted to feel safe, I would sleep in her room.

Her floggings affected my schooling. I've had exams I couldn't complete because of whatever happened the night before. One time she beat me so badly, I had wails on my skin. I had welts, wails and belt marks which prevented me from completing my swimming exam. Back in High School we had to change for swim class, but I couldn't do it because I couldn't take my clothes off. There was a clear belt mark on every part of my body. There was a belt mark wrapped around my hand. I was heavily covered up because I didn't want them to know. Instead, I lied to the teacher and told them I was on my menstrual cycle. I said I didn't want to swim, when really, it was the bruises and wails on my skin that I didn't want anyone to see.

My step-dad and my sister were around when the abusive incidents occurred, because they lived with us, and they basically told my mom "No, this is wrong, you can't be having parties like this while your daughter is upstairs sleeping and men are going upstairs to the bathroom." They fought about it and my brother, sister and step-dad called her some names. The only thing she kept saying was "Well if you guys don't like it, call the police." That was her favourite sentence. "You don't like it. Call the police. Call the police. Lock me up, lock me up!"

I think she knew and I'm pretty sure she would have known that everything she did to me was wrong. But she did what she wanted, when she wanted. She was definitely not one of those parents who would acknowledge that she was doing something wrong and say, "Okay I'm gonna stop." She had no chill. Always doing what she wanted and that was that.

There was abuse both ways. My mom didn't have a care in the world when it came to relationships. She didn't have any loyalty to anyone; she was not loyal to me as a parent, and when she got older she was not loyal to any man. Call what you will, infidelity or cheating- I watched it all growing up.

If ever I did look good as a kid, it was because the people around me made *sure* I didn't look like what I was going through. My step-sister would comb my hair and buy me clothes. Whenever I didn't eat dinner, she would get me ready and take me out with her to buy food. As a kid I just saw that as "Oh my God, you're getting me food." I wasn't aware that my mother refusing to feed me was a form of abuse. My grandmother always had this house rule that we were not to walk around and talk about the things that went on inside the home. So my step-sister reminded me about how my mother would spend the money that the government would send for me and my siblings, during the summer, or during the Christmas holiday. She would spend on them but, she would give me hand –me-downs, and just put little to no effort in anything she did for me. As I now know, she didn't like me because of my father, so she used to abuse me by inflicting trauma on me. Moreover, whatever relationship she had with my grandmother would be passed down to me.

    I can recall one incident when all my siblings got brand new snow gear for the winter. I needed a jacket and every day I would go to school with a jacket that had a hole in it, because my mom would still let me wear it. "Oh, you're going to wear it till it runs out and you're not getting a new one, blah, blah, blah." It got to the point where I got really, really sick. My step-sister took all the money that she had and she really didn't have a lot of money at the time, but she bought me a whole winter wardrobe. My mom didn't care. She didn't care if I wore socks with snow boots or whether I had a hat to wear. These are things that other people would make sure were in place.

My mom did a lot, more than the physical, mental and emotional- she also plotted to turn my siblings against me. She was so good at doing that; she would always skew the facts and spin the narrative, telling my sister all sorts of things. Amidst all of these unfortunate events, I found the strength to start fighting back. As I got older, I started to fight back.

One day we got into an argument. I grabbed a hold of her and she grabbed me by my neck. She kept squeezing my neck, and at that point, I could have sworn that I took my last breath. I had nothing left and I was just trying to save my own life. It was either me or her. I was a child and she was a grown woman who had already lived her life, so she shouldn't have been trying to cut mine short. Her hand was on my neck and she kept pushing and pushing. By this time, I could feel a part of my throat was crushing; my windpipe was crushing. So I tried to grab her hand to release it from my neck. That wasn't working because she had a firm grip. So I'm like, okay, what else can I do? Then it came to me.

I took one of my hands and put it down by my side. Then I moved my feet apart, wrapped my feet around her and tripped her. She either fell towards the stairs, fell down the stairs or fell on the ground- I didn't really care. She called everybody in Jamaica accusing me of trying to kill her. I would always be the aggressor whenever she told the story. In her words, "Me bring yuh come here, so me can tek yuh out!" She tried to do this quite a few times, and when I would fight back, she would run and say "Dis pickney put har hand on me. She's cursed." She's this, she's that." Back home in Jamaica, no one wants to hear that you put your hand on your mom. Not once did she tell anybody the truth. In an explanation to my grandmother, I told her I couldn't just allow her to continue to squeeze my throat. I had to fight back.

CHAPTER 7

LENGTH OF ATTENTION

I can vividly see everything that has happened to me even as I share my story. So if you asked me to illustrate it, I could draw every little detail exactly the way it happened.

The punishment I received was definitely different, way different. She hit us, but if she ever did anything to my siblings, it would be a simple punishment. My treatment was far more extreme. There were some weird things she would do to me and it could be for the smallest thing. She did what we refer to in Jamaica as "Lay Wait" for me. Sometimes it is as if she punished me in bulk, because sanctions piled up and were imposed on me, for things like not washing the dishes. She would allow things to build up and then one day everything would come out.

She punished my sister but it was never to the extreme where my sister felt captured or caged. My sister was free to do whatever she wanted. She got to live life more than I did. So I posed the question to my mom, "We're both girls, why are you so hard on me and not her?" "Oh, I don't trust your colour. I don't trust your kind. You're very sneaky, you're conniving." She would call me "This likkle Red Pickney." Everything had to do with my complexion. It was just too weird. It didn't matter what it was. She did not care. Whenever someone walked up to her and said, "Your daughter is so beautiful," she'd get mad.

Once she told me "Oh, yuh tink yuh skin colah a guh bring yuh any weh? Ongle a white man a guh want yuh." I never forgot the day. "A likkle white man, an' unnuh a guh tek drugs an' him a guh breed yuh an' lef' yuh!"

When I started dating, my boyfriends would come over to the house and she would interrogate them. *"Yuh sure you want fi date dis likkle gyal?"* You know seh she nasty and nuh love bade?" Weh yuh waan deh wid deh wid har fah, yuh see how long it tek har fi put on har clothes?" Look how long it took her to do this." All of that crap in an effort to sabotage my friendships and relationships. She was so conniving. She would say I would have to bring my siblings on the date-crazy stuff like that. If I didn't complete whatever she wanted me to do, then it was to hell with whatever I wanted to do. Basically it was "Cinderella" syndrome.

She never stopped and she did not care. She was telling people that I was barren, that she had seen my test results from my doctor, and that I couldn't have kids. She would embarrass me in front of my friends at my house. She just didn't care. So when I met my fiancé I never brought him around at first. Eventually, when she got the chance, she would tell him things about me to try to make him leave me. She would say "She has a learning disability. Are you sure you want to take that upon yourself?" Her goal is to cause people around me to hate me- including my fiancé. I just don't know what she's capable of doing anymore.

To be honest, if my mom and I reconciled before I wrote this book, I would have no plans to write. I would have kept it all. I would have died with all of these things in my heart. And I gave her that choice. I told her. I said, "We can forget about all the stuff you put me through, what you did to me over the years. I'll forget it. All I want you to do is have a relationship with me. I just want you to love me." She told me straight up, "No." I would do anything in my power to make sure I hear my daughter's voice at night, and to be sure that I'm still in God's grace with her. My mom did not give a shit.

She told me that she went to see a doctor once. It wasn't an actual doctor or someone who knew science. This is my truth and I have nothing to say to her after this. Whatever my mom needed to do to be able to hurt me, she would do. It could have been through my siblings, or it could have been through anything that I had. Whenever we got into arguments she would say, "Yuh lucky seh yuh deh yah enuh, me shudda dash yuh weh. Me siddung inna di clinic and a tink bout fi just kill yuh and get on wid me life!" She said a lady came to her and told her, "This is not the route you want to go with your child." Apparently that lady had many abortions. Her advice to my mother was, "Carry your child and be proud to carry your child." In the past, I used to think that she should have just aborted me because it's not worth what she put me through.

Before my grandmother passed away, my mom sent me a voicemail that I still have to this day. She basically told me that my grandmother was dead. So I stopped working, left early and didn't even tell my workplace that I was leaving. I walked right off the site in shock. I hurried home and told my family that I had to go by my grandmother.

This was the situation; I heard she had just died. Then she texted me back after I told her that I was on my way to see my grandmother. She said, "Oh, just kidding, she's right here."I was like," What is wrong with you?" The only reason she did that was because she wanted to get me to come to her house and talk. I came to find out my grandmother was still living and breathing just fine at home. I thought "What is wrong with you? What really…what is wrong with you?" She said, "Oh so that's what it took for you to run. That was it? That's what it took for you to come see me or be by your grandmother's side? I had to lie to you and tell you she's dead?" I'm like, "Why would you even think to say something like that?"

Eventually I resolved that I still wanted to be loved by her despite everything she's done to me. Everyone was looking at me thinking, "Are you sick? When is enough, enough?" My excuse was, "Well, she's my mother. I'm still supposed to care for her, still supposed to love her."I question God every day, "Why, why am I like this?" People hurt me and usually most people would say, "Okay that's it" and walk away. But I'm not like that. I'm not that person. Knowing everything she's done, I never once let it phase me. I still showed up to her anniversary party. I used to look at it like this; we're a family and yes we may be dysfunctional, but we're working through it. I always looked at her as my mom and still loved her. At some point I would have still wanted her to be around and be part of my life. It just didn't work that way and it got to the point where I was finished asking. I left it right there.

I said all of this to her and told her that all I ever wanted was to be loved. Every parent gives out some type of punishment when their kids do something wrong. Sure you can punish them, but they should still be loved. My thing with my mom is this: all those years she didn't speak to me, she went to sleep every night not knowing if anything was wrong with me. Not knowing if I was dead or alive. I thought to myself, you hated me so much that if someone came and said "Christine is this or that" you didn't care. In my opinion, that's not love. I understand two people can get into an argument and tempers flare, feelings get hurt, but I'm her daughter.

There was a time when I had gotten into an argument and I would have to seek refuge at the pastor's house. I couldn't sleep at the pastor's house because he was afraid that my mom would react and risk him losing his licence- which she would. She is very much capable of doing things like that.

She didn't want people to reach out and help me. Even when I moved out of her house, she held onto my I.D. I had to call the police and tell them that I needed my I.D. They called her and they said, "It's not yours, you need to give it up whatever the heck you guys are going through. You have to give it back to her." And I remember I went there with the cops to get my I.D. because I did not trust her. She has been taking things out in my name with my credit.

I don't even know who she really is or who she can be compared to. It's hard to say because she doesn't have the qualifications to be a mother. That title should have been taken from her years ago. Now she's supposed to assume the role of a grandmother. I told her, *"When it comes to me and you, I don't want anything from you. There's nothing you can do for me or say to me. All you need to do is play your part as a grandmother. Excel in that department. Everything that I went through is all lost and all forgiven."* And she didn't even want to take that opportunity. I gave her the choice. I said *"We can pretend like this never happened."* I was willing to do that. *"All you need to do is just be a grandmother and stop with the little things that you do- like trying to attack me, my spirit and everything that I am. Just stop."* She told me straight up, she said "No. You don't know what I went through with you."

I want to say to both my parents: I went through a lot- between surviving suicide, not knowing where I truly belonged, or what my purpose was. I just had to look at it as something that happened. All this happened, it's in the past, and I basically had to train myself to feel and think independently. I developed a higher level of consciousness, and acknowledged that yes, these two people are my parents, but this is their character and they are not going to change. So I'm either going to sit there and keep knocking at the door while no one answers, or I'm going to knock and wait for an answer-and if nobody answers I am just going to keep moving forward. I had to move on with my life.

I was still growing up, and thankfully, my life experiences did not stop me from maturing and becoming an adult. I still had to live my life and go through the typical struggles. I had to come to a resolution; my mom's not there, my dad's not there. But I have something that I will always be grateful for, and that is the other people who filled that void along my path.

Along the way I've had great friendships. I've been friends with one of my friends for over twelve years. We got close near the end of High School. We've been close for a long time, and she has helped me grow as a person-especially when it came to being a mother. Being timid as a first time mother, she helped me believe in my task ahead. I wanted to embody what she did, as I watched her raise her daughter. Both her and my aunt are great examples of motherhood.

They epitomize what it means to be a great mother and what it means to really love your kids.

My other friend is older than I am; she's like a mother and sister all in one, and she keeps me grounded. She's very helpful when it comes to my daughter, my relationship, and to me as a person. She's always there when I need her.

Honestly, I may not have a great deal of friends, but I have a closely knit group of about seven friends who keep me grounded. If it wasn't for them, I don't know where I'd be. There are times where it gets rough, but these friends know all my moves- my highs and my lows. We've had our differences, but I just cherish the fact that they're so real at the end of the day. Even when the road gets bumpy and there are hurdles, they've always told me to never give up. "Keep at what you're doing." Whenever it comes to my daughter, my relationship or even with myself sometimes, and I feel like giving up- I just call them. They're always right there. They help me get out of whatever is holding me bound. They say, "We're going to help you feel better about yourself again, going to help you feel at one with whatever you went through." Because of their support, my obstacles no longer affect me. They may still be there but they can't hurt me anymore.

CHAPTER 8

MEN BEFORE YOUR CHILDREN

When I hear "church" my heart starts beating so rapidly and I feel like something just takes over. I feel like I'm in a dark hole all over again- similar to what I went through with the passing of my grandmother. I'm still not over it. I still wish she was here. That's the main reason why I haven't even blessed my daughter at church yet, because it is so hard to step foot in there. I wish that she could have seen this book; she is the reason I wrote it.

My grandmother took me to church and I volunteered in various capacities. I had some expertise when it came to reciting a Bible verse or organizing quizzes and games. It was for the youth arm of the church, so there were different things I took on, like evangelism.

I got baptized because of my grandmother. I did a lot with her before she passed, and shared a lot of memories with her like going to church. I'm very grateful for them, but I miss them. These were all things that moulded me. My grandmother always reminded me that no matter what troubles and trials I endured, I should always have God. She always taught me to never turn my back on Him. It doesn't matter what you are going through, or who is around you; you do not give up on God. When she passed I felt like that. I felt like what was the point? She was a Christian herself and I didn't understand why her? What was she called for or where does it leave me? So I did a lot of the blaming. I asked "Why me, why not?" It still hurts because she's not here. But I'm slowly learning to accept it.

My grandmother had three children; my mom and her two brothers. She has many grandchildren and great grandchildren. She also had sister and brothers, which would be my grand aunts and uncles. I've never spoken to any of them since the funeral. I believe that when it comes to a death in the family, the different generations within the family are supposed to step up and keep the family together. I've never had an aunt or an uncle call and say, "Hey how are you doing? How's your daughter?" As the matriarch of my family these are things that my grandmother would do. Now, it's just all lies, and I don't have time for the lies with the family.

On my dad's side I've never met my grandmother although I've spoken to her on the phone. She lives in Grenada but she has seen pictures of me. I don't know her at all. What I do know is that relatives on that side of the family would comment and say how much I resembled her whenever I was at family reunions. They would say how much I remind them of her because of the traits that I have of her. "You walk to your grandmother's storms" is what they would say. I want to know my family roots, so I told my sister that one day we should go there for a visit.

I met my grandfather very briefly. I was at the mall that I used to visit regularly, and in the food court I would always see this old man. One day I was introduced to him. I never knew the whole time I was going there, as a kid in my early teens, that that man was my grandfather. I've never really spoken to him, but I've seen him.

There are two grandmothers on my mom's side; my mom's mother and my sister's dad's mother.

My relationship with my brothers is on and off, but the relationship with my sister-which is my mom's daughter-is very good. I feel like the only reason why it became stronger is because she became a mother. If she wasn't a mother, we would fight like cat and dog. She didn't agree with anything I was doing, especially when it came to my daughter. So now that she's a mother, we can share certain ideas, likes and dislikes about our children and other stuff. You could say we're on the road to recovery because we've been through a lot.

In a perfect world, I would want her to know what really happened with our mom. My mom always picked me; even when we were growing up she was already warped by my mom. To this day, she is still trying to get me and my mom to reconcile. She keeps using the fact that I have a daughter and that I am a mom to ask me what the right thing to do in this situation is. It's just not going to work. So I don't even want to begin to talk about the things that our mother has done to us, because she's always going to choose her at the end of the day. It would make no difference.

Let her think what she wants. I don't want her to hear it from me. On occasion, she would speak out about a few things that my mom has done, but at the same time she still wants that whole family portrait- even though I told her to let it go.

It is late for apologies. It's very late because if she attempts to apologize now after this book is released, it's not going to change how I feel about her. It would have had an impact if I was sixteen years old, and when I was young, broken and had time to fix things. We could have tried then. I am twenty-nine years old now. It's over, there's nothing more I can do. I've tried everything: counselling, talking to her directly, and I took her out to dinner. We've even done family dinners; it always just ends up in a big war.

I end up storming out of the house because I want to do something to her. It's not going to work and I wish all my siblings the best of luck when it comes to my mom. That woman has a way of twisting people to get them to do things for her. She is still toying with people even at her ripe age of …48, 49, 50 years old…I don't even know anymore. I've blocked that out of my mind.

Right before I cut her off, she called me and asked, "Like how yuh nuh chat to me, me a guh tek yuh name offa me insurance den?" I'm like, "What kind of question is that for you to pick up the phone and ask me?" She just wanted my reaction or she wanted attention. Even when she passes away, it's not going to change anything.

I called my sister because I thought it was too much. "Why would she even say that?" she asked. I hung up the phone and my mom continued to text me asking the same thing. So I just blocked her. But before I did, I just told her to do whatever she wanted to do. If you're going to remove my name, then just do it. It's always something. In the past, she always knew how to get me to run back to her arms. She really thought that I would say, "No, no, no, leave it there."

One thing I refused to replicate was my mom's history of always putting men before me. She always put men before her children. She always had a distasteful preference. There was a particular ex-boyfriend who kicked me out of the house because she let him. This was all because I didn't want to do the laundry in the pouring rain. He told her I had no manners and she should kick me out to teach me a lesson. And she let him. So I was outside in the wet, cold pouring rain without a jacket; crying, screaming, and kicking the door so they could let me back in. I told them I'd do anything. They turned off the lights and went to bed. So I took the bus to my ex-boyfriend's house and stayed there for two nights.

In my mind I thought, you could not be this horrible of a mother. It was always one thing after another. There was never a balance for me, no break in transmission. It was not like she did this on a Sunday and then one day she took me to the park. No it was always something.

She had one of her partners beat me with a dog leash, an actual dog leash. My skin was wailed. My mother told him when he came home that I was mouthing off, and he suggested that I had a different kind of punishment. What happened was she asked me to wash the dishes, and I replied, "No you wash them!" He chased me all the way to the basement cellar, and even when I yelled, "Stop, stop, no it hurts!" he continued. He said, "Your mom is the boss, you should listen to her!" How does this make sense? Even if it's not my own child, I would never give another man an opportunity to put his hands on that child. I don't care what it is. As a man you come to me and tell me. Then I will punish the child if necessary.

My mom was not like that. She gave every man in her life that autonomy. "They're your step-dad." Step-dad was allowed to beat us. Step-dad was allowed to tell us whatever. One time I went for a visit and her ex-husband- who I will never forget, was arguing with me. He proceeded to throw hot tea on me. I had to call my boyfriend down to the house to get me out of there. I shook and the whole house shook; I saw red. I told him straight up, "If that tea touches my skin you're not going to have time to call 911. If you throw that tea, by the time I'm done with you, you'll be in a body bag.

Of course, she took the man's side and told me not to talk to her because I was rude and mouthed off to her now ex-husband. Even if I did, what does that have to do with him wanting to burn me with hot tea? What would be the sense in defending a man over your own child, who eventually leaves and is now your ex? I would have had to be on the road to recovery as my skin healed and he'd still be gone, out of the picture.

Her husband now is the worst. I tried to stay away from her and him. The shit that he says to me, to her about us; he approves of the way she deals with us. He tells her "Your kids can't come to the house. This is my house now. Let them come here and you'll see." She follows every order he gives her.

He tried to fight my sister a couple of weeks ago. I told my sister, "You're either telling me for two reasons: you want me to do something about it or you just want to vent." My sister knows if I go down there and I step foot in that house, the house is crumbling. I'll crumble - my mother, her husband and anything else there.

My mom knows exactly what she's doing. Getting into an argument with my sister who is obviously going to call me, will lead to one thing- pulling up to the house. That was what she wanted. She is conniving but she's very smart. She knows every move I will make and what move I won't. However, now that I shut her out, she can't program my next move anymore; there's no connection. Even if she hears something, it's not by me.

For years, I let her control me even when it concerned my relationship, because to be honest, I wanted her to love me so badly. It was sickening. Back then, I didn't care what she did. If she told me "I'm going to make food. Do you want something? Are you hungry?" I'm looking at her like, "Yeah mom I'm coming to your house" as if nothing happened. I'd block out everything she did, every word she said, just to be beside her. Back then, not now. That chapter of my life is over.

When I started my counselling, I even considered her. I called her and I said, "Hey you know, it's going to get to the point with my counselling where they're going to want my mom to step in and do a session with me…" She told me straight up, "Fix yuhself before yuh fix me." In my head, I'm like, "What?!" I told my counsellor that it's just not going to work. We would have to forget about the possibility of having her in a session because she was not going to.

My brothers and sister can go by the house, but it's always an argument. So my sister goes there, but she knows very well that her visit will result in either one of two things: she'll leave totally pissed off or she will just never set foot there again. My sister goes there but my brother lives there. The same brother that lives there is the same brother I bailed out of jail.

I've done so much even though they are the parental figures. My brother lives with my mom, however, I'm responsible for his freedom. I put the money up for his bail. My mom told me on the phone straight up, "I am not doing this; I don't have… no, I'm not putting my money into your brother." In my head I'm like, "You're not supposed to look at it like that. He's your kid."

He's been charged as an adult, and we're not talking about little charges, we're talking about serious charges. He could have been gone for ten years or more. So what were we going to do? She said she didn't care, so I called the lawyer and made a financial arrangement. I was going to save this child. Till this very day, I am my little brother's surety. The only reason why he's out is because of me, and he lives at my mom's house because of me. My mom tried to overturn that arrangement and remove my name off the bail bond.

She wants to have control over his life because that is what she is used to. When she stood surety for him once or twice, she would call the police on him for stupid things like not taking out the garbage or not doing the dishes. She was used to pulling his bail. I told my brother, "I'll pay your bail, just abide by my rules and my conditions." I don't need anything from him. I would say, "Let me know when you're going on probation." Right now my brother goes to counselling through my networking and guidance.

I'm still helping even though I said I wouldn't. It's always a hand out situation with our mother- she always wants something. Her son is safe at home and is not locked up. A normal person would recognize that I am still here; I still care. However what I do always goes unnoticed. Her husband even told her that he would divorce her if she bailed out my brother, and she's willing to comply because she's broken and damaged.

We've tried to get her to go to counselling but she's never attended. It's not just counselling with me. She says nothing's wrong with her. Last time I told the doctor that she said, "Nutten nuh wrong wid me. Me A'rite, just like everybaddy else weh yuh know." ["There's nothing wrong with me. I'm fine. I'm as normal as any other person you meet."] *'Very normal. Very, very.'*

CHAPTER 9

WHERE IT ALL BEGAN

"What is wrong with your child?" is a question I would call and ask my grandma on the phone when she was alive. She would try to reason with my mom. There was history with her and my grandmother, and I knew that. My grandmother left my mom in Jamaica at a young age, and my great-grandmother would abuse her. I heard it all. My thing with my mom is, I understand if childhood abuse skewed your thought process, but seek help. You should have sought help before you had a child. After this happened to you, you could have got help and that would have made you a better mother. You would have a better understanding of who you are as a woman, and what you're about to experience- which is motherhood.

When you find out you're about to become a mother, there is a specific feeling in your stomach, and you change. Your entire focus shifts from yourself to your child. You no longer wonder about how you're going to eat, instead you think about what your child is going to eat. It's really not about you anymore, it's about your child. She did not.

As a baby, my grandmother told me she showed me nothing but love. My grandma lived with us at that time and she is the one who gave me my full name. So my mom didn't name me, my grandmother did. I was her first granddaughter, and to be honest, if someone had not told her that my mother went into the hospital to give birth to her first granddaughter, she would not know.

My grandma and my mom had a disagreement so my mom kept it from her. My grandmother dropped everything to be by my side, and by my mom's side, even during their little argument. She basically told me she made it work because of me.

"I stayed. I knew how your mom was. I knew everything about her, but I made it work because of you." That's what my grandmother said. "You're my first grandchild, and I wanted to be there. I didn't want to be just a phone call away, I wanted to be there." She always helped me. It even put a wedge between me and my sister because she believes that my grandmother loved me more than she loved her. I've explained to her that it has nothing to do with who she loved more. When you have your first child, it's a different type of bond. Whenever we were younger and we would argue, I would tell her, "Well, you had the mother that I wanted and I had the grandmother you wanted.

She would literally hide me from people. People didn't even know I existed. One day when I did come outside or when you did see me, I would hear, "Wait, you have another daughter?" "I didn't even know that." People come up to me, "OH, that's your mother?" "Yes." "That's your daughter?"

She did some cruel things like making me go hungry as punishment. I had to bear the law, which was her law. Whenever bad stuff happened to her, she'd take it out on me. So let's say a man rejected her, she would take that out on me. She would say, "It's because of you, that men don't want me no more." As a kid, I'm just like, "What does it have to do with me?"

She's always putting men before her children. The reason could be that she was submissive to men and seeking attention from everywhere and in every form. Therefore if it came in the form of a man telling her to distance herself from her children, a family member or a friend, she would conform. Her mentality is still one of infancy.

She has even told guys about me. I'm actually convinced that she probably tried to sell me up against men once or twice. I had to wonder what man was coming to her next. Every man that she brought into her life always took a liking to me. Some were like father figures and didn't agree with things that she did. But then she had other men that were still young themselves and didn't care.

I was talking to my aunt and I was explaining how I don't think anybody really understands the hatred I have toward my mother. But now that you read the book, you'll understand why I am the way I am. I was telling her, I don't think the hatred I have for my mom will ever go away. And she agreed with me. She's like, "I know. I told your mom years ago that her kids are going to grow up resenting or even hating her if she doesn't fix up." And I told her it was past fixing or mending.

I just want her to go away, but I want her to see my success and I want her to crash and burn because of it. Like I want her to know: You can't have anything because you've damaged who I am before I even became who I am. So I don't feel like you should sit on the same stool or the same chair as me, or at the same table when I'm out there. She shouldn't be around when I'm talking to these young kids or when my book is on a TV show. She should not have any benefits at all.

My grandmother would say, "Hell hath no fury like a woman scorned." "The way that you were scorned, even if your mom was to write out I'm sorry on a thousand pages and letters, it's not going to take away your pain. Your pain has to go away because you want it to go away."

CHAPTER 10

GUARDIAN ANGEL

At her husband's birthday party, my mother just pretended like nothing had happened, although both of us knew the real story. She forced me to remove my grandmother from her home, so she did not have to be bothered with caring for her own mother at her husband's event. My mother booked a specialised mobility vehicle to make the transfer. My fiancé and I had to lift her out of the taxi, into our building and up through the elevator. We made her as comfortable as possible, even though I knew it was wrong of my mother. My grandma had a visible look of shame and disgust because of her daughter's actions.

Whenever she's around people, she makes it seem hunky dory. "Oh, I love my daughter, I'll do anything for her." It gets to the point where she can make people think anything. Nobody knows me. To everyone's knowledge she has four kids, but they've never seen me because I was never around. So when people meet me now, in some cases for the very first time, they go "Oh my God, this is your daughter? She's so beautiful, she looks just like you." I believe it would stir up things in her. She'd respond and be like "Yeah!" People just don't know that I exist.

Someone reached out to me the other day and when they asked me my last name, they repeated it and asked me if my mother is "so-and-so." After I concurred, they said, "Oh my God, you're the daughter she talks about that gives her nuff problems." In my head, I'm like, *I give her problems?* So I just basically had to tell the person I don't deal with her and I don't know what she told you, but it's all a lie. In retrospect, I may have acted out at times. It would be normal for any child to act out, but I wasn't treated as just any child, I was treated horribly by her.

Then she tells people that I have no manners and that I ran away. Again, in my head I'm like, *I ran away?* I wish that was one of the things I did. I wish I had the nerve to run away. I did not run away. She kicked me out and then spun the narrative to make it seem like she was the victim.

When that person DM'ed me on Instagram and told me things that my mother would say about me, I just laughed. She said, "I really can't believe this is your mother." They used to be friends and she says she cut my mother off. So if you're her friend and I'm her daughter, and everything I'm saying matches up with what you're saying, then we are not in the wrong.

She told me my mom said so many things about me. She would sit there and be like, "No your daughter is wicked. Why would she put you through that?" So I gave her a bit of the story, and in my head, I'm like *wow, now you know the truth.* Her friend or her ex-friend needed to know that my mom is not who she thought she was; she is a great pretender and a great liar.

My mom can make you believe anything. She would tell you like she told everyone in Jamaica, that I threw her down the stairs, but she didn't tell anybody that she nearly crushed my whole larynx and took away my life. She never told anybody that she broke a dish over my head. All the facts would be conveniently left out of her story just to make her appear to be a superior grandparent, which she never was. So I just left it all.

So many people come to me and say, "You're her daughter?" Oh my God, you look just like your mom." When my daughter gets older and someone looks at her and remarks, "You're much prettier than your mom" I would be surprised. I want that to be the case because she is my child. However, my mom did not like that. It made her envious. When people said that to her, you could tell that it hurt her.

Everyone knows that my mom was in some sort of competition with me. I didn't understand why a grown woman would want to be in competition with her own daughter.

She is always doing things to receive attention so as to seem like a perfect parent. She is not and after everything she put me through, she did not even make an apology. "No regrets" is her mantra and she has shown no remorse.

Every time that I've spoken to her about things that she did, all she keeps saying is that *she did what she needed to do to make me have a better life*. Over the phone, I told her "if this is what you think a better life is, then I do not want to see you at your worst." I did not have a better life because of her. I'm twenty-nine years old and at this age I should have had way more experience. I should have been doing a lot more, but you hindered me from doing a lot. I thought I was incapable of being a mother. I definitely didn't think somebody was capable of loving me, or that I would be able to love somebody.

I was robbed of my childhood. My mother robbed me of my childhood. She took every bit of peace and happiness I should have had. I believe that your happiest moments should occur when you are a child. Whenever I hear other people's stories and they say "I was nothing but a happy child, my parents love me", I know I don't have the same story. The reason why my story is different from a lot of people is because not one but both parents followed the same path.

I'm twenty-nine years old. She's forty and going on four grandkids now; she hasn't changed. Not an ounce of change in that woman. She is the way she is and that's just how she is. I feel like if she had counselling and all the things that I'm doing to help me heal, maybe it would be a start.

We had some counselling sessions in the past. We've had people step in to try to mend our relationship. At one point, we had someone who used to come every week and conduct regular checks between me and my mom. We had Children's Aid in our life for a good amount of time. One of the programmes our mom had to do was act like she was the perfect mom but she wasn't.

The only thing that happened was that she would benefit from all the little coupons and the little groceries, but what did she really do with it? She was still trying to fight me which was really punishing me and abusing me. She still didn't change. There was a time when she was vulnerable and she would open up and say what she went through with her mom and dad may have caused a regressive pattern. I just think she didn't really care.

Even to this day, she still talks about me with my sister and I've cut her off completely. I can't see what she's doing and she really can't see what I'm doing. Yet she's still trying to find a way to tear me down but my mom and my sister have their own stories. As my sister would say, my mom was not in any shape or form based on how she was with us. Anyways, she gave my sister more experiences and paid more attention to her. She used to tell my sister that black is beautiful and she would tell me "Your colour is not wearing again, it's washed out."

My step-sister reminded me that my mom made me eat dog food one time. If there was ever a time in my life that I could highlight as a good moment with my mom, it would probably be as a baby. Because I would have no memories as a baby but for as long as I can remember, I have no fond memories of my mother. The early pictures of me and my mother would seem like such a perfect family, so beautiful.

Little did people know, I wanted to claw out her face and she wanted to claw out mine.

We went to dinner and I told her, "I do not want you to really even give me an apology. I just want you to acknowledge that you did these things, and your acknowledgement will be a step to help us move forward." My mom would eat the food and belch at the dinner table and be like, "I never did any of these things; you're lying." She is a big time narcissist, she's a manipulator, she's conniving, and she's evil.

My dad taunts me like my mother. Just recently there was an incident where I had to emerge from the shell I was in because I had blocked him, but then something happened and I totally went off on him.

When it comes to my parents, I consider them the same. No one outshines the other. They are in the same league. My dad is doing the same thing my mom has always done, which is not taking responsibility for his actions. He has ten of us; we're all living proof of him. His words to me in our recent communication was that I am a mistake and by far the worst of all of his children. He also said that I should be mentally institutionalized.

Yeah he's so bitter, way past bitter. He spoke about my relationship. He spoke about my child. I told him to say whatever he wanted, because there is not much that I have to say to him. "I am going to say to you what I have to say to you when it comes to my life, but it is because you said something about my child who is, to be honest your grandchild." I just unleashed everything on him; I couldn't back. I made sure to tell him *"what and what not"* he should crawl back up into.

I told him, *"The next time you hear about me, it's either going to be on your deathbed or in a grave because I don't understand how not just you but both you and my mother can put me through so much. And it's like it doesn't come to your head mentally as a person; like when is enough, enough? You trashed my name, you've trashed my image. You've done so much. You've tried to hurt me through other people. When do you say, honestly, this game is boring? Let me pick another person, let me find another game. No, you guys don't. You guys think my life is a game, but my life is not a game. And even if it is, I control the game, I'm rolling the dice. Not you guys. You guys gave birth to me and yes, I may be a product of you guys, but I'm not of you guys. And I think that's what's just killing you guys, because I've made something out of myself. Like that hole that you guys said that I would be in, I'm not in. That person that you said would never love me, I have. That mental disability that you guys say I have and I can't really do much with, I have done something with it; hence, this book. Clearly you guys don't know about it." I* just went off. I went off on him.

He knows he can never pick up the phone and call me because number one, I'm not going to answer. Two, I'll have nothing but curse words to say to him. So he picked a fight with my sister and he told her things that he actually wanted to tell me. And because she called me and told me these things, the message was received. Two things I'm serious about: Don't play with me about my child or my family. He really wanted to hear from me so badly.

As I told my sister he really wanted to hear from me, so I gave him what he requested. On that one fateful day, I let him have it. He didn't even answer the phone, so I left everything on the answering machine. I told him everything that was on my mind and that I was thinking about. I sent the message and just left it there.

Prior to that he was getting only bits and pieces, little pieces from me. But I never really unleashed everything for him, so that day he got it all. Everything - a half hour voice message left on his answering machine.

CHAPTER 11

SUPER HERO

From my heart and soul, I had to embody every aspect of heroism in my unconditional love as a mother. When my daughter said "Mommy" for the first time, it was the most indescribable moment and it was heart-warming to receive that coveted title from her. Just knowing that she looks up to me as her protector, role model, the one who guards her and keeps her safe is a great responsibility and one that I treasure always. As a mother, there is a difference between raising other kids like when I took care of my brothers and sister, and now raising my own.

She looks to me for everything and that special bond we share was created by God. I made sure to do this job to the best of my ability. I would speak to my friends who are already moms and get ideas on the best steps to take and different methods to use as a new mom. That coupled with my experience in child care from when I was younger and all that my grandmother taught me; I will forever uphold my vows to be better than the mother that raised me.

It's not just my relationship with my daughter, but many people trust me with their kids-my best friend with my goddaughter and my sister with her son. They already know the dynamics of my life, who I am as a person and how much I care for these kids. The way I see it now as an adult, is that I have overcome all these traumatic events that have happened in my life. We're all going to age, so it's either those life situations will come back to haunt you, or we can use them and turn them around for positive change for others.

As my daughter grew from a baby to a toddler, we had many precious moments. I used to watch her roll around before she learned to walk and take her first steps. Feeding time was a treat for both of us, and I enjoyed teaching her words as she formed her speech. Every moment with her is all worth it. I will always be by her side and I wouldn't change being her mom for the world.

Daddy's Girl

To be honest my daughter is definitely a daddy's girl. From the time she was a baby and you can't tell her otherwise. Her dad is like her Superhero. He is so good with her.

My Soul mate Fiancé

I met my fiancé when I was eighteen, and he was a safe haven for me. He was there for me during certain situations- the trauma, abuse and everything with my mom. I didn't think our friendship would turn into what we now share today as a couple, but it did and it was as though God ordained it to be. At first I kind of ran from that. I basically told him I wasn't interested in having the kind of relationship that we currently have. It is not what I was looking for initially. We dated and we had fun, but eventually our relationship blossomed and God put us together.

We met through a friend through Black Berry Messenger (BBM). It was the era of BlackBerry Messenger. After we started talking, there was a connection. So we met up and went on a couple of dates. He realized that there was a connection between us before I did. I mostly tried to run from those emotions.

My fiancé experienced the death of a cousin who was really close to him, and he was trying to process and deal with that loss. He said he looked up to the heavens, praying that

God would send him someone who was just for him and didn't want much. Right after his cousin passed he met me. What really drew me to him were the things he did- and in my experience they weren't normal. We would talk for hours on the phone and then when I fell asleep, he would make sure to wake me up so that I could get ready for school. I was struggling to graduate and he would affirm me and constantly remind me, "You can do this!" Yeah, it was the little things. He was very supportive.

When I had to move back in with my mom, he offered to let me stay with him. In the midst of the trauma I was going through with my mom, he told me that we should move in together. I told him no, that it was too much too soon, and that I really thought it would be better for us to get to know each other for a bit longer before making that move. He constantly reassured me through his actions and made me feel safe. He would always check up on me to see how I was doing. All these qualities in him were exciting to see. He made me realize my beauty, not just my physical beauty, but the actual person that I am.

We have had our obstacles like any normal couple would have. We are not perfect. We both have our flaws, but there is great value in what we share and we are still together. I had to learn to let go and allow things to play out and transform into what we are today. Once again, I wasn't looking to be in a relationship with anyone. As a matter of fact, I wasn't even looking to have fun. Because of the sheltered life I lived, I was still caged psychologically. Many of the things I had the opportunity to experience were because of him.

My learning disability was never something he judged me about. He always said that he believes everyone has a learning disability of some sort, because there is always going to be something that someone does not know how to do. With him I had better conversations and I learned how to better formulate sentences. Also he took away my fear of individuals who were always trying to get at me, stir me up or rouse me in anger. He helped me understand that not everybody was trying to hurt me, and he encouraged me to give them a chance and open up more to people. This was reminiscent of the things my grandmother would teach me, so he came along at the right time in my life. All of that history, and then the progress we've made taking on the role of parents with a family of my very own, blows my mind.

CHAPTER 12

PRIDE STRENGTH & LOVE

I find there's an advantage to anything I do. Because of what I have endured, I am more of a keen listener. When my customers are speaking, I pay attention and when it comes to my mental health work, I listen to understand. So when a customer is frustrated, I know in the back of my mind that the customer is not frustrated with me, they are frustrated with the company. I don't make it about me or take it personally. If someone is angry with me, I know how to process certain emotions and feelings. What I have noticed with people is that not everybody says exactly what they mean, or means what they say- especially if they are emotional.

I developed this whole thing as a child and now use this as an adult; how to decipher people's emotions. I know that the problem that is initially stated is not the primary or underlying issue- it is just the tip of the iceberg. My job is to break down the iceberg and figure out what is underneath. So I listen to the frustration. Being the Superhero that I am, I always like to help. I'm always helping people. So if I can't help you, my job is not complete. I will figure out ways for you to get the help you need.

As a mother, I do have my times though. I want people to know that having a learning disability, being a mother and going through all these events causes me to have times when I don't want to do anything. I need my time alone. My daughter knows, and she calls it 'Mommy Time'. I'll sit there and ponder about how I can do better. I do not ever want my daughter to look back and say "Mommy caused me to miss out on that one book and now I don't know how to read." Whatever I don't know how to do, I make the effort to learn, just for her.

It is paramount to me that I pay attention to every little thing she does. If it is a new toy, I get into that new toy, if it is a new show, I get into it. I make things fun, but at the same time I am strict. I value certain things, like family time. I want to ensure she becomes something in life, and is not told she will not amount to anything like I was.

Too often I was told that I was not going to achieve success, and no one would love me because I had all these disadvantages. I had an anger problem, I had a learning disability, and I didn't know how to form a conversation. Those voices were always playing on repeat in the back of my head. The only person that did believe in me wholeheartedly was my grandmother. If I told her I wanted to be a lawyer or doctor- as silly as it sounded- she was like "child you can do anything you want to do. I will be here." She was a mentor and I also had my aunt.

It has been rough with my fiancé because of communication struggles. He said that he believes that I do not open up and he believes that I am very sheltered. He would compare me to the likes of a time ticking bomb for an adequate description. As a child I was scared to say certain things, I was scared to open up. Now, as an adult, I am not afraid to open up. I am fearless. If I feel like you're doing me wrong, or you're doing something that hurts me I can advocate for myself. Skilfully, I can say exactly what is on my mind and lead the conversation so you understand that I am hurt. No more taking bull crap from people. Even with my fiancé, if we get into an argument where he threatens to leave, because of the way I was raised, I am emotionless. I do not care. I would be like "What are you telling me that for, I don't care." So he calls me cold-hearted.

In order to live my best life I have to cut off the poison around me- which is my mother, father and anyone else who wants to be added to that list. To truly live my life, I needed to write this book. I had to get this weight off my shoulders because it was killing me. By writing this book, I would get the load off my shoulders, and put down this cross that I have been carrying for almost twenty-nine years. Not only that, but I could also heal. I know that I went through all of these things and overcame them. I have overcome the abuse of my mother, I have overcome the abuse by my father and I have overcome all these situations and obstacles. I now have the tools to successfully ensure a quality life for myself and secure a future for my child.

No matter what I face in life, in the back of my mind I remind myself that in everything I do, or anything I touch, do it with love. I don't have any animosity. I'm not mad. If I didn't go through these situations in my life, I do not feel like I would be the person I am today. I would probably be that scared little girl and I would be afraid to jump. Now I am jumping and I am writing this book.

My grandmother would tell me, "You are always a diamond; you always have a pure heart." The rainbow always represents me carrying on, because rain or shine, you're going to see a rainbow. The diamond is me discovering who I really am; whatever I went through, I still remained strong and pure in heart.

At the end of the day she is my mother and I can not take that away from her. I want her to know that just because I forgive her, does not mean I forget.

And at the end of this book, I want all my offenders to know, if I do forgive you, I forgive you, and I'm moving on. I'm just going to leave that here, like, right there."

If you guys think this is all of me, where I started to where I am now, just know the best is yet to come. This Unique Cut Diamond has many more colours to unfold.

www.ingramcontent.com/pod-product-compliance
Lightning Source LLC
Chambersburg PA
CBHW072157200426
43209CB00079B/1977/J